DICTIONARY DATA STRUCTURE: THEORY AND APPLICATIONS WITH PYTHON AND TKINTER

VIVIAN SIAHAAN
RISMON HASIHOLAN SIANIPAR

Copyright © 2024 BALIGE Publishing

All rights reserved. No part of this book may be reproduced, stored in a retrieval system, or transmitted in any form or by any means, without the prior written permission of the publisher, except in the case of brief quotations embedded in critical articles or reviews. Every effort has been made in the preparation of this book to ensure the accuracy of the information presented. However, the information contained in this book is sold without warranty, either express or implied. Neither the authors, nor BALIGE Publishing or its dealers and distributors, will be held liable for any damages caused or alleged to have been caused directly or indirectly by this book. BALIGE Publishing has endeavored to provide trademark information about all of the companies and products mentioned in this book by the appropriate use of capitals. However, BALIGE Publishing cannot guarantee the accuracy of this information.

Published: MAY 2024
Production reference: 0300524
Published by BALIGE Publishing Ltd.
BALIGE, North Sumatera

ABOUT THE AUTHOR

Vivian Siahaan is a highly motivated individual with a passion for continuous learning and exploring new areas. Born and raised in Hinalang Bagasan, Balige, situated on the picturesque banks of Lake Toba, she completed her high school education at SMAN 1 Balige. Vivian's journey into the world of programming began with a deep dive into various languages such as Java, Android, JavaScript, CSS, C++, Python, R, Visual Basic, Visual C#, MATLAB, Mathematica, PHP, JSP, MySQL, SQL Server, Oracle, Access, and more. Starting from scratch, Vivian diligently studied programming, focusing on mastering the fundamental syntax and logic. She honed her skills by creating practical GUI applications, gradually building her expertise. One particular area of interest for Vivian is animation and game development, where she aspires to make significant contributions. Alongside her programming and mathematical pursuits, she also finds joy in indulging in novels, nurturing her love for literature. Vivian Siahaan's passion for programming and her extensive knowledge are reflected in the numerous ebooks she has authored. Her works, published by Sparta Publisher, cover a wide range of topics, including "Data Structure with Java," "Java Programming: Cookbook," "C++ Programming: Cookbook," "C Programming For High Schools/Vocational Schools and Students," "Java Programming for SMA/SMK," "Java Tutorial: GUI, Graphics and Animation," "Visual Basic Programming: From A to Z," "Java Programming for Animation and Games," "C# Programming for SMA/SMK and Students," "MATLAB For Students and Researchers," "Graphics in JavaScript: Quick Learning Series," "JavaScript Image Processing Methods: From A to Z," "Java GUI Case Study: AWT & Swing," "Basic CSS and JavaScript," "PHP/MySQL Programming: Cookbook," "Visual Basic: Cookbook," "C++ Programming for High Schools/Vocational Schools and Students," "Concepts and Practices of C++," "PHP/MySQL For Students," "C# Programming: From A to Z," "Visual Basic for SMA/SMK and Students," and "C# .NET and SQL Server for High School/Vocational School and Students." Furthermore, at the ANDI Yogyakarta publisher, Vivian Siahaan has contributed to several notable books, including "Python Programming Theory and Practice," "Python GUI Programming," "Python GUI and Database," "Build From Zero School Database Management System In Python/MySQL," "Database Management System in Python/MySQL," "Python/MySQL For Management Systems of Criminal Track Record Database," "Java/MySQL For Management Systems of Criminal Track Records Database," "Database and Cryptography Using Java/MySQL," and "Build From Zero School Database Management System With Java/MySQL." Vivian's diverse range of expertise in programming languages, combined with her passion for exploring new horizons, makes her a dynamic and versatile individual in the field of technology. Her dedication to learning, coupled with her strong analytical and problem-solving skills, positions her as a valuable asset in any programming endeavor. Vivian Siahaan's contributions to the world of programming and literature continue to inspire and empower aspiring programmers and readers alike.

Rismon Hasiholan Sianipar, born in Pematang Siantar in 1994, is a distinguished researcher and expert in the field of electrical engineering. After completing his education at SMAN 3 Pematang Siantar, Rismon ventured to the city of Jogjakarta to pursue his academic journey. He obtained his Bachelor of Engineering (S.T) and Master of Engineering (M.T) degrees in Electrical Engineering from Gadjah Mada University in 1998 and 2001, respectively, under the guidance of esteemed professors, Dr. Adhi Soesanto and Dr. Thomas Sri Widodo. During his studies, Rismon focused on researching non-stationary signals and their energy analysis using time-frequency maps. He explored the dynamic nature of signal energy distribution on time-frequency maps and developed innovative techniques using discrete wavelet transformations to design non-linear filters for data pattern analysis. His research showcased the application of these techniques in various fields. In recognition of his academic prowess, Rismon was awarded the prestigious Monbukagakusho scholarship by the Japanese Government in 2003. He went on to pursue his Master of Engineering (M.Eng) and Doctor of Engineering (Dr.Eng) degrees at Yamaguchi University, supervised by Prof. Dr. Hidetoshi Miike. Rismon's master's and doctoral theses revolved around combining the SR-FHN (Stochastic Resonance Fitzhugh-Nagumo) filter strength with the cryptosystem ECC (elliptic curve cryptography) 4096-bit. This innovative approach effectively suppressed noise in digital images and videos while ensuring their authenticity. Rismon's research findings have been published in renowned international scientific journals, and his patents have been officially registered in Japan. Notably, one of his patents, with registration number 2008-009549, gained recognition. He actively collaborates with several universities and research institutions in Japan, specializing in cryptography, cryptanalysis, and digital forensics, particularly in the areas of audio, image, and video analysis. With a passion for knowledge sharing, Rismon has authored numerous national and international scientific articles and authored several national books. He has also actively participated in workshops related to cryptography, cryptanalysis, digital watermarking, and digital forensics. During these workshops, Rismon has assisted Prof. Hidetoshi Miike in developing applications related to digital image and video processing, steganography, cryptography, watermarking, and more, which serve as valuable training materials. Rismon's field of interest encompasses multimedia security, signal processing, digital image and video analysis, cryptography, digital communication, digital forensics, and data compression. He continues to advance his research by developing applications using programming languages such as Python, MATLAB, C++, C, VB.NET, C#.NET, R, and Java. These applications serve both research and commercial purposes, further contributing to the advancement of signal and image analysis. Rismon Hasiholan Sianipar is a dedicated researcher and expert in the field of electrical engineering, particularly in the areas of signal processing, cryptography, and digital forensics. His academic achievements, patented inventions, and extensive publications demonstrate his commitment to advancing knowledge in these fields. Rismon's contributions to academia and his collaborations with prestigious institutions in Japan have solidified his position as a respected figure in the scientific community. Through his ongoing research and development of innovative applications, Rismon continues to make significant contributions to the field of electrical engineering.

ABOUT THE BOOK

In the dynamic realm of Python programming, dictionaries stand out as one of the most versatile and efficient data structures available. This book delves deep into the full potential of Python dictionaries, exploring their fundamental operations, practical applications, and their pivotal role in data science, software development, and graphical user interface (GUI) design using Tkinter.

Dictionaries in Python are analogous to real-world dictionaries; they consist of key-value pairs that provide a fast and straightforward way to store and manage data. Unlike lists or arrays where elements are accessed via their position, dictionaries allow for quicker access through unique keys, making them indispensable for handling large datasets where speed and efficiency are crucial.

The early chapters of this book introduce the basic operations associated with dictionaries, such as adding, removing, and modifying items. Each concept is reinforced with clear, practical examples demonstrating how these operations are used in everyday coding tasks. We also delve into more complex dictionary methods that enhance functionality, such as get(), keys(), values(), and items() methods, which facilitate efficient data retrieval and manipulation.

As we progress, the book explores advanced applications of dictionaries in Python, including their use in web development for managing data, configuring settings in applications, and handling feature management in machine learning algorithms. The versatility of dictionaries is also showcased in tasks like JSON data parsing and management, where dictionaries' ability to nest and store complex data structures is particularly beneficial.

One of the highlights of this book is the integration of dictionaries with Python's powerful libraries for data analysis and visualization, such as Pandas and Matplotlib. This includes examples of converting dictionaries into Pandas DataFrames to simplify data analysis tasks, or using dictionaries to store data points for graphical representation.

Moreover, we introduce the development of graphical user interfaces using Tkinter, where dictionaries play a critical role in managing the state and properties of GUI elements. You will learn how to dynamically update GUI components based on user interactions stored and manipulated through dictionaries. This not only enhances the functionality of your applications but also showcases the synergy between data management and interface design.

In addition to practical applications, the book addresses the performance aspects of dictionaries, comparing their efficiency with other data structures in Python. This discussion extends into real-world scenarios, demonstrating how dictionaries can be optimized for performance and memory usage in large-scale applications.

We also examine common pitfalls and best practices when working with dictionaries to help you avoid common errors and improve the readability and efficiency of your code. From simple tasks like populating a dictionary with data, to more complex scenarios involving dictionaries within dictionaries, this book provides you with the knowledge to use dictionaries effectively in your programming projects.

Lastly, this book doesn't just teach you how to use dictionaries; it inspires you to think more deeply about data structuring and management. By integrating dictionary operations with Tkinter GUI development, you will gain a comprehensive understanding of how these tools can be combined to create more interactive and user-friendly applications. Whether you are a data scientist, a backend developer, or a software engineer, mastering dictionaries and Tkinter will enhance your coding toolkit and open up new horizons in your software development career.

CONTENT

BASIC OPERATIONS — 1
INTRODUCTION — 1
BASIC OPERATIONS — 1
Example 1.1 Hotel Reservation System — 3
Example 1.2 GUI Tkinter for Hotel Reservation System — 5
Example 1.3 Contact Book Application — 8
Example 1.4 GUI Tkinter Contact Book Application — 11
Example 1.5 Restaurant Menu Management System — 14
Example 1.6 GUI Tkinter for Restaurant Menu Management System — 16
Example 1.7 E-commerce Shopping Cart System — 20
Example 1.8 GUI Tkinter for E-commerce Shopping Cart System — 22
Example 1.9 Retail Inventory Management System — 25
Example 1.10 GUI Tkinter for Retail Inventory Management System — 26
Example 1.11 Event Registration System — 29
Example 1.12 GUI Tkinter for Event Registration System — 31
Example 1.13 Retail Sales Report Generation — 34
Example 1.14 GUI Tkinter for Retail Sales Report Generation — 36
Example 1.15 Electronics Store Inventory System — 38
Example 1.16 GUI Tkinter for Electronics Store Inventory System — 41

ADVANCED OPERATIONS — 45
INTRODUCTION — 45
Example 2.1 Sales Analysis System — 46
Example 2.2 GUI Tkinter for Sales Analysis System — 48
Example 2.3 Combining Customer Data — 51
Example 2.4 GUI Tkinter for Combining Customer Data — 53
Example 2.5 Managing Configuration Settings — 56
Example 2.6 Tkinter for Managing Configuration Settings — 58
Example 2.7 Session Management in a Web Application — 61
Example 2.8 GUI Tkinter Session Management in a Web Application — 63
Example 2.9 E-commerce Application Customer Preferences — 66
Example 2.10 GUI Tkinter E-commerce Application Customer Preferences — 68
Example 2.11 Counting Item Occurrences in Store Inventory — 71
Example 2.12 GUI Tkinter Counting Item Occurrences in Store Inventory — 73

ADDITIONAL OPERATIONS AND FEATURES	76
Example 2.13 Real-Time Inventory Tracking System	77
Example 2.14 GUI Tkinter for Real-Time Inventory Tracking System	79
Example 2.15 Implementing a Role-Based Access Control (RBAC) System	82
Example 2.16 GUI Tkinter for Implementing a Role-Based Access Control (RBAC) System	84
Example 2.17 Merging Customer Data from Multiple Sources	87
Example 2.18 GUI Tkinter for Merging Customer Data from Multiple Sources	89
Example 2.19 Setting Up a Voting System	92
Example 2.20 GUI Tkinter for Setting Up a Voting System	94
Example 2.21 Sorting a Product Inventory by Sales	97
Example 2.22 GUI Tkinter for Sorting a Product Inventory by Sales	99
Example 2.23 Sports League Ranking System	101
Example 2.24 GUI Tkinter for Sports League Ranking System	103
Example 2.25 Using Hashable Objects for Efficient Data Retrieval and Manipulation	106
Example 2.26 GUI Tkinter for Using Hashable Objects for Efficient Data Retrieval and Manipulation	108
Example 2.27 Caching Function Results with Hashable Inputs	111
Example 2.28 GUI Tkinter for Caching Function Results with Hashable Inputs	113
Example 2.29 Shared Configuration Settings	116
Example 2.30 GUI Tkinter for Shared Configuration Settings	119
Example 2.31 Web Application Session Management	122
Example 2.32 GUI Tkinter for Web Application Session Management	123
MORE ADVANCED OPERATIONS	127
Example 2.33 Word Frequency Analysis in a Document	129
Example 2.34 GUI Tkinter for Word Frequency Analysis in a Document	131
Example 2.35 Ranked-Choice Voting System	134
Example 2.36 GUI Tkinter for Ranked-Choice Voting System	136
Example 2.37 Network Traffic Monitoring System	139
Example 2.38 Tkinter for Network Traffic Monitoring System	141
Example 2.39 Building an Inverted Index for Document Search	144
Example 2.40 GUI Tkinter for Building an Inverted Index for Document Search	146
Example 2.41 Transportation Network Analysis	149
Example 2.42 GUI Tkinter for Transportation Network Analysis	151
Example 2.43 Software Package Dependency Resolver	154
Example 2.44 GUI Tkinter for Software Package Dependency Resolver	157
Example 2.45 Handling Configuration Data for a Distributed System	160
Example 2.46 GUI Tkinter for Handling Configuration Data for a Distributed System	162
Example 2.47 E-commerce Transaction Analytics	166
Example 2.48 GUI Tkinter E-commerce Transaction Analytics	168

SCIENTIFIC APPLICATIONS — 171

INTRODUCTION	171
Example 3.1 Pairwise Sequence Alignment	171
Example 3.2 GUI Tkinter for Pairwise Sequence Alignment	173
Example 3.3 Air Quality Analysis and Visualization	177
Example 3.4 GUI Tkinter for Air Quality Analysis and Visualization	180
Example 3.5 Gene Expression Analysis Across Different Conditions	183

Example 3.6 GUI Tkinter for Gene Expression Analysis Across Different Conditions	185
Example 3.7 Analyzing Signal Data from Multiple Sensors	188
Example 3.8 GUI Tkinter for Analyzing Signal Data from Multiple Sensors	191
Example 3.9 Handling Parameter Tuning	194
Example 3.10 GUI Tkinter for Handling Parameter Tuning	196
Bibliography	**307**

BASIC OPERATIONS

INTRODUCTION

In Python, a dictionary is a built-in data type that stores data in a key-value pair structure. Dictionaries are mutable, meaning they can be changed after their creation. Each key-value pair in a dictionary is separated by a colon :, with the key on the left and the value on the right. Keys must be unique within a dictionary and need to be of a type that is immutable (e.g., strings, numbers, or tuples that contain only immutable elements). The values can be of any data type.

BASIC OPERATIONS

Here are some of the fundamental operations that can be performed with dictionaries in Python:

Creating a Dictionary:

```
my_dict = {"name": "Alice", "age": 25, "city": "New York"}
```

Accessing Elements:
You can access elements using their keys.

```
print(my_dict["name"])   # Outputs: Alice
```

If you try to access a key that does not exist, Python will raise a KeyError.

Adding and Updating Elements:
Adding a new key-value pair or updating an existing key can be done using the assignment operator.

```
my_dict["email"] = "alice@example.com"   # Adds a new key
my_dict["age"] = 26   # Updates the existing key
```

Removing Elements:
You can remove elements using several methods:
pop(key): Removes the item with the specified key and returns its value.

```
age = my_dict.pop("age")
```

popitem(): Removes the last inserted key-value pair (as of Python 3.7; before that it removed a random item).

```
item = my_dict.popitem()
```

del statement: Deletes an item or the entire dictionary.

```
del my_dict["city"]
del my_dict   # Deletes entire dictionary
```

Checking for a Key:
Use the in operator to check whether a key exists in the dictionary.

```
"name" in my_dict # Returns True
```

Getting Length:
Use the len() function to find out how many key-value pairs are in the dictionary.

```
len(my_dict)
```

Iterating Through a Dictionary:
You can iterate through keys, values, or key-value pairs:

```
for key in my_dict:
    print(key)

for key, value in my_dict.items():
    print(key, value)

for value in my_dict.values():
    print(value)
```

Example 1.1
Hotel Reservation System

Creating a dictionary in Python can be very useful for various real-world applications across different domains. Here's a comprehensive example demonstrating how to use a dictionary to manage and process data in a hotel reservation system.

In this example, we will design a simple system for managing hotel room bookings. The system will use dictionaries to store information about hotel rooms, guests, and bookings.

Overview of the System

The hotel has multiple rooms, each with different attributes such as room type, rate per night, and availability. Guests can book rooms based on their preferences, and the system will keep track of which guest is in which room and for how long.

Step-by-Step Implementation

1. Define the Room Data: Create a dictionary to hold details about each room in the hotel.

```
rooms = {
    101: {'type': 'Standard', 'rate': 100, 'available': True},
    102: {'type': 'Deluxe', 'rate': 150, 'available': True},
    103: {'type': 'Suite', 'rate': 200, 'available': True},
    104: {'type': 'Standard', 'rate': 100, 'available': True},
    105: {'type': 'Deluxe', 'rate': 150, 'available': True},
}
```

2. Manage Bookings: Use another dictionary to track which room is booked by which guest.

```
bookings = {}
```

3. Define Functions for Handling Bookings:
- Function to check room availability and book a room.
- Function to release a room when a guest checks out.

```python
def book_room(room_id, guest_name):
    if rooms[room_id]['available']:
        rooms[room_id]['available'] = False
        bookings[room_id] = {'guest': guest_name}
        print(f"Room {room_id} is now booked by {guest_name}.")
    else:
        print(f"Room {room_id} is not available.")

def checkout_room(room_id):
    if room_id in bookings:
        guest = bookings.pop(room_id)
        rooms[room_id]['available'] = True
        print(f"{guest['guest']} has checked out. Room {room_id} is now available.")
    else:
        print(f"No booking found for room {room_id}.")
```

4. Interact with the System:
- Booking rooms for different guests.
- Checking out and making rooms available again.

```python
book_room(101, "John Doe")
book_room(103, "Alice Smith")
checkout_room(101)
```

4. Display Current Bookings and Room Status:
Displaying the status of each room and current bookings can help in managing the hotel more effectively.

```python
def display_status():
    print("Room Status:")
    for room_id, info in rooms.items():
        print(f"Room {room_id} ({info['type']}): {'Booked' if not info['available'] else 'Available'}")
    print("\nCurrent Bookings:")
    for room_id, info in bookings.items():
        print(f"Room {room_id}: Booked by {info['guest']}")

display_status()
```

Benefits of Using Dictionaries in This Example
- Efficiency: Dictionaries provide fast lookup, insertion, and deletion operations, which are ideal for real-time booking systems.
- Flexibility: The structure of dictionaries makes it easy to add more properties to rooms or bookings, such as adding amenities to rooms or storing check-in and check-out dates for bookings.
- Simplicity: Using dictionaries simplifies data management, making the code easier to understand and maintain.

This simple hotel reservation system showcases how dictionaries can effectively manage related data, making them invaluable for backend processes in software applications. This approach can be expanded or modified to fit more complex systems or other domains such as inventory management, event scheduling, and more.

Example 1.2
GUI Tkinter for Hotel Reservation System
To build a rich graphical user interface (GUI) using Tkinter, which allows users to interact with the hotel room booking system as described in your code snippet, we'll use a class-based approach to encapsulate the functionality and provide a clean, user-friendly interface.

Below, We'll provide a detailed explanation of creating a Tkinter GUI that manages room bookings, checks room status, and handles room check-outs.

Step 1: Setup the GUI Class Structure
First, we initialize the main window and set up the basic class structure for the Tkinter GUI.

```
import tkinter as tk
from tkinter import ttk, messagebox, simpledialog

class HotelApp:
    def __init__(self, master):
        self.master = master
        self.master.title("Hotel Room Booking System")
        self.master.geometry("500x300")

        self.rooms = {
            101: {'type': 'Standard', 'rate': 100, 'available': True},
```

```python
            102: {'type': 'Deluxe', 'rate': 150, 'available': True},
            103: {'type': 'Suite', 'rate': 200, 'available': True},
            104: {'type': 'Standard', 'rate': 100, 'available': True},
            105: {'type': 'Deluxe', 'rate': 150, 'available': True},
        }
        self.bookings = {}

        self.setup_widgets()

    def setup_widgets(self):
        ttk.Label(self.master, text="Hotel Booking System").grid(row=0, column=1)

        # Booking button
        ttk.Button(self.master, text="Book Room", command=self.gui_book_room).grid(row=1, column=0)

        # Checkout button
        ttk.Button(self.master, text="Checkout Room", command=self.gui_checkout_room).grid(row=1, column=2)

        # Status display area
        self.status_text = tk.Text(self.master, height=10, width=50)
        self.status_text.grid(row=2, column=0, columnspan=3)
        self.display_status()

    def book_room(self, room_id, guest_name):
        if self.rooms[room_id]['available']:
            self.rooms[room_id]['available'] = False
            self.bookings[room_id] = {'guest': guest_name}
            messagebox.showinfo("Success", f"Room {room_id} is now booked by {guest_name}.")
        else:
            messagebox.showerror("Error", f"Room {room_id} is not available.")
        self.display_status()

    def checkout_room(self, room_id):
        if room_id in self.bookings:
            guest = self.bookings.pop(room_id)
            self.rooms[room_id]['available'] = True
            messagebox.showinfo("Success", f"{guest['guest']} has checked out. Room {room_id} is now available.")
        else:
            messagebox.showerror("Error", f"No booking found for room {room_id}.")
        self.display_status()

    def display_status(self):
        self.status_text.delete(1.0, tk.END)
        self.status_text.insert(tk.END, "Room Status:\n")
        for room_id, info in self.rooms.items():
```

```python
            self.status_text.insert(tk.END,    f"Room    {room_id}    ({info['type']}): 
{'Booked' if not info['available'] else 'Available'}\n")
        self.status_text.insert(tk.END, "\nCurrent Bookings:\n")
        for room_id, info in self.bookings.items():
            self.status_text.insert(tk.END,    f"Room    {room_id}:    Booked    by 
{info['guest']}\n")

    def gui_book_room(self):
        room_id = simpledialog.askinteger("Book Room", "Enter room ID:")
        guest_name = simpledialog.askstring("Book Room", "Enter guest name:")
        if room_id and guest_name:
            self.book_room(room_id, guest_name)

    def gui_checkout_room(self):
        room_id = simpledialog.askinteger("Checkout Room", "Enter room ID:")
        if room_id:
            self.checkout_room(room_id)

# Run the application
if __name__ == "__main__":
    root = tk.Tk()
    app = HotelApp(root)
    root.mainloop()
```

Explanation of the Code

- Class Definition (HotelApp): This class handles the initialization and layout of the GUI. It sets up the main window and the interactive widgets for hotel room booking and management.
- Hotel Room Data: The rooms and bookings are stored in dictionaries, making it easy to manage availability and booking status.
- Widget Setup (setup_widgets): Widgets include labels, buttons, and a text display area. Buttons trigger dialogues to book or checkout rooms, while the text area displays the current status of all rooms and bookings.
- Booking and Checkout Methods: Methods book_room and checkout_room handle booking and checking out logic, respectively. These methods also call display_status to update the text display area with the latest room and booking statuses.
- Display Room and Booking Status: display_status updates the text display to show the availability of each room and current bookings.
- Graphical User Interface Dialogs: gui_book_room and gui_checkout_room provide interfaces for the user to input room IDs and guest names using dialog boxes.

Features of the GUI
- Dynamic Updates: The GUI updates the room status in real-time as bookings are made or rooms are checked out.
- User Feedback: Uses message boxes to inform the user of successful actions or errors (e.g., trying to book an unavailable room).
- Simplicity and Usability: The GUI is straightforward, making it easy for users to interact with the system without extensive training.

This application demonstrates a practical implementation of a hotel booking system using Python's Tkinter module, highlighting how GUI applications can effectively manage and interact with data structures like dictionaries.

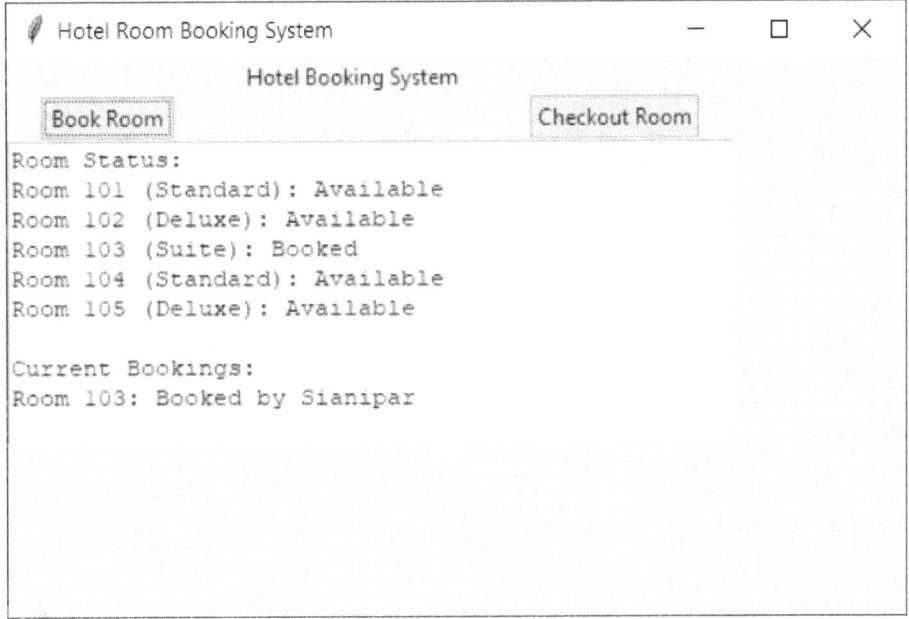

Example 1.3
Contact Book Application

In the real world, dictionaries in Python are incredibly versatile and can be used for a variety of applications where data needs to be stored and accessed efficiently. A common scenario where accessing elements in a dictionary becomes crucial is in managing a contact book application.

Scenario

Imagine you're building a contact book application where users can store and retrieve contact details like phone numbers, email addresses, and physical addresses. The application utilizes a dictionary to hold this information, with each contact's name as a key, and another dictionary as the value to store various details.

Example Setup

Here's how the contact book might be structured using a Python dictionary, and how you might access various elements to retrieve or update contact information:

```python
# Initialize the contact book as a dictionary
contact_book = {
    "John Doe": {
        "phone": "555-0101",
        "email": "johndoe@example.com",
        "address": "123 Elm St"
    },
    "Jane Smith": {
        "phone": "555-0202",
        "email": "janesmith@example.com",
        "address": "234 Oak St"
    }
}

# Accessing a specific contact's details
def get_contact_details(name):
    if name in contact_book:
        return contact_book[name]
    else:
        return "Contact not found."

# Example usage of accessing elements
print(get_contact_details("John Doe"))  # Retrieve John Doe's contact details

# Output:
# {'phone': '555-0101', 'email': 'johndoe@example.com', 'address': '123 Elm St'}

# Updating a contact's phone number
def update_phone(name, new_phone):
    if name in contact_book:
        contact_book[name]["phone"] = new_phone
        return f"Updated {name}'s phone number to {new_phone}."
    else:
        return "Contact not found."

# Update phone number for Jane Smith
```

```python
print(update_phone("Jane Smith", "555-0303"))

# Adding a new contact
def add_contact(name, phone, email, address):
    if name not in contact_book:
        contact_book[name] = {
            "phone": phone,
            "email": email,
            "address": address
        }
        return f"Added new contact {name}."
    else:
        return "Contact already exists."

# Add a new contact
print(add_contact("Alice Johnson", "555-0404", "alicejohnson@example.com", "345 Pine St"))

# List all contacts
def list_contacts():
    return list(contact_book.keys())

# Get all contact names
print(list_contacts())

# Output:
# ['John Doe', 'Jane Smith', 'Alice Johnson']
```

Explanation:

- Dictionary Structure: The contact_book uses each person's name as a key. Each key maps to another dictionary that contains the phone, email, and address as keys with respective values.
- Accessing Details: Using the name, you can quickly retrieve any contact's full information (get_contact_details). This is efficient because dictionary lookups by key are very fast.
- Updating Information: Similarly, you can update the phone number for any contact by accessing the nested dictionary directly (update_phone).
- Adding New Contacts: New entries can be added to the dictionary as long as the name doesn't already exist in the keys, thus preventing duplicates.
- Listing Contacts: You can list all the contacts by accessing the dictionary keys, which will give you the names of all the contacts stored.

This example demonstrates how dictionaries allow for efficient storage, retrieval, and manipulation of structured data, making them ideal for applications like a contact book where quick access and updates are frequently needed.

Example 1.4
GUI Tkinter Contact Book Application

To create a rich graphical user interface (GUI) in Tkinter using the contact book operations, we'll develop a Python application encapsulated within a class structure. This GUI will enable users to interact with the contact book by adding, updating, and viewing contact details.

Step 1: Import Tkinter and Define the GUI Class

First, we'll import necessary Tkinter modules and set up the main class which will initialize the GUI and bind the contact operations.

```python
import tkinter as tk
from tkinter import ttk, messagebox, simpledialog

class ContactBookGUI:
    def __init__(self, master):
        self.master = master
        self.master.title("Contact Book GUI")
        self.master.geometry("400x300")

        self.contact_book = {
            "John Doe": {"phone": "555-0101", "email": "johndoe@example.com", "address": "123 Elm St"},
            "Jane Smith": {"phone": "555-0202", "email": "janesmith@example.com", "address": "234 Oak St"}
        }

        # Setting up the user interface
        self.setup_ui()

    def setup_ui(self):
        self.label = ttk.Label(self.master, text="Contact Book", font=('Arial', 16))
        self.label.pack(pady=10)

        # Buttons
        ttk.Button(self.master, text="Add Contact", command=self.add_contact).pack(pady=5)
        ttk.Button(self.master, text="Update Phone", command=self.update_phone).pack(pady=5)
```

```python
        ttk.Button(self.master, text="View Details", command=self.view_details).pack(pady=5)
        
        # Display area
        self.text_display = tk.Text(self.master, height=10, width=50)
        self.text_display.pack(pady=10)

    def add_contact(self):
        name = simpledialog.askstring("Add Contact", "Enter the contact's name:")
        if name in self.contact_book:
            messagebox.showerror("Error", "Contact already exists.")
            return
        phone = simpledialog.askstring("Add Contact", "Enter the contact's phone number:")
        email = simpledialog.askstring("Add Contact", "Enter the contact's email:")
        address = simpledialog.askstring("Add Contact", "Enter the contact's address:")
        self.contact_book[name] = {"phone": phone, "email": email, "address": address}
        messagebox.showinfo("Success", f"Added new contact {name}.")

    def update_phone(self):
        name = simpledialog.askstring("Update Phone", "Enter the contact's name:")
        if name not in self.contact_book:
            messagebox.showerror("Error", "Contact not found.")
            return
        new_phone = simpledialog.askstring("Update Phone", "Enter the new phone number:")
        self.contact_book[name]['phone'] = new_phone
        messagebox.showinfo("Success", f"Updated {name}'s phone number to {new_phone}.")

    def view_details(self):
        name = simpledialog.askstring("View Details", "Enter the contact's name:")
        details = self.contact_book.get(name, "Contact not found.")
        self.text_display.delete('1.0', tk.END)
        if isinstance(details, dict):
            info = f"Name: {name}\nPhone: {details['phone']}\nEmail: {details['email']}\nAddress: {details['address']}"
        else:
            info = details
        self.text_display.insert(tk.END, info)

# Main function to run the application
def main():
    root = tk.Tk()
    app = ContactBookGUI(root)
    root.mainloop()

if __name__ == "__main__":
    main()
```

Explanation of the Code:
1. Class Definition (ContactBookGUI):
   This class encapsulates all GUI elements and functionalities. It initializes the main window (master) and sets up the contact book.
2. setup_ui Method:
   This method sets up the user interface, including labels for titles, buttons for operations (adding, updating, and viewing contacts), and a text display area for showing contact details or messages.
3. Contact Operations (Add, Update, View):
   - add_contact: Opens a dialog to input new contact details. It checks for duplicates before adding a new contact.
   - update_phone: Allows updating the phone number of an existing contact after verifying that the contact exists.
   - view_details: Retrieves and displays the details of a specified contact in the text area.
4. Interaction with Tkinter Widgets:
   - Dialogs (simpledialog) are used to input data from the user.
   - Message boxes (messagebox) provide feedback based on the outcome of operations.
   - The text display area (Text) shows the details of the contacts when requested.

Features of the GUI:
- Dynamic Interaction: The GUI responds dynamically to user inputs and updates the internal state of the contact book accordingly.
- Error Handling: Provides error messages for invalid operations, such as attempting to update a non-existent contact.
- Clear User Feedback: Users receive clear, immediate feedback on the actions they perform via dialog messages and the text display area.

This application is a straightforward example of how a GUI can be used to manage a simple database-like system, providing intuitive interactions for users through graphical elements.

Example 1.5
Restaurant Menu Management System
In real-world applications, dictionaries are extensively used for their flexibility, easy access, and efficient management of data. Here's a detailed example that demonstrates adding and updating elements in a dictionary in a restaurant management system. This system handles the menu and daily specials, allowing restaurant staff to add new items and update existing ones easily.

Scenario
Imagine a restaurant that has a digital menu system, allowing staff to dynamically add new menu items or update existing ones, such as changing prices, descriptions, or ingredients based on availability and chef decisions.

System Setup
1. Initial Menu Setup:
The restaurant menu is initially set up as a dictionary with categories as keys (like 'Starters', 'Main Courses', 'Desserts') and each category containing another dictionary of dishes and their details.

```
menu = {
    'Starters': {
```

```
        'Spring Rolls': {'price': 5.99, 'ingredients': ['cabbage', 'carrot', 'garlic']},
        'Garlic Bread': {'price': 3.99, 'ingredients': ['bread', 'garlic', 'butter']}
    },
    'Main Courses': {
        'Steak': {'price': 15.99, 'ingredients': ['beef', 'salt', 'pepper']},
        'Salmon': {'price': 12.99, 'ingredients': ['salmon', 'lemon', 'dill']}
    },
    'Desserts': {
        'Ice Cream': {'price': 4.99, 'ingredients': ['milk', 'sugar', 'flavoring']},
        'Cake': {'price': 4.99, 'ingredients': ['flour', 'sugar', 'eggs']}
    }
}
```

2. Adding a New Menu Item:

Function to add a new dish to a category. If the category does not exist, it will create a new category.

```
def add_menu_item(category, dish_name, price, ingredients):
    if category not in menu:
        menu[category] = {}
    menu[category][dish_name] = {'price': price, 'ingredients': ingredients}
    print(f"Added {dish_name} to {category} with price {price}.")

# Example of adding a new starter
add_menu_item('Starters', 'Bruschetta', 4.99, ['bread', 'tomatoes', 'onion', 'basil'])
```

3. Updating an Existing Menu Item:

Function to update details of an existing dish. It can handle updates in price or ingredients.

```
def update_menu_item(category, dish_name, new_price=None, new_ingredients=None):
    if category in menu and dish_name in menu[category]:
        if new_price:
            menu[category][dish_name]['price'] = new_price
        if new_ingredients:
            menu[category][dish_name]['ingredients'] = new_ingredients
        print(f"Updated {dish_name} in {category}.")
    else:
        print(f"{dish_name} not found in {category}.")

# Example of updating a dish's price
update_menu_item('Main Courses', 'Steak', new_price=17.99)
```

Explanation
- Adding Items: The add_menu_item function checks if the specified category exists. If not, it creates a new category and then adds the new dish and its details.
- Updating Items: The update_menu_item function updates specific aspects of an existing dish, such as its price or ingredients. If the dish or category does not exist, it outputs an error message.
- Dictionary Operations: These functions effectively showcase how dictionaries can be utilized for managing structured data where keys can dynamically map to complex information sets.

Benefits of Using Dictionaries
- Efficient Data Access and Modification: Dictionaries provide O(1) average time complexity for lookups, insertions, and deletions.
- Flexibility: Easily add new categories or modify existing data without impacting other parts of the menu.
- Scalability: Capable of scaling to handle larger data sets such as a full-service restaurant menu with multiple sections.

This system could be part of a larger application interfacing with a database or a front-end user interface, providing restaurant staff a quick and easy way to keep their service offerings up-to-date.

Example 1.6
GUI Tkinter for Restaurant Menu Management System

To create a comprehensive graphical user interface (GUI) using Tkinter for managing a restaurant menu, we'll design a class-based application that allows users to interactively add and update menu items, and view the current menu. This system will help restaurant staff to manage menu items more efficiently.

Step 1: Define the GUI Class
We'll start by setting up the main class for our GUI. This class will handle the creation of the GUI components, interactions, and tie these actions back to our menu management functions.

```
import tkinter as tk
```

```python
from tkinter import ttk, messagebox, simpledialog

class MenuManager:
    def __init__(self, master):
        self.master = master
        self.master.title("Restaurant Menu Manager")
        self.master.geometry("600x400")

        self.menu = {
            'Starters': {
                'Spring Rolls': {'price': 5.99, 'ingredients': ['cabbage', 'carrot', 'garlic']},
                'Garlic Bread': {'price': 3.99, 'ingredients': ['bread', 'garlic', 'butter']},
                'Bruschetta': {'price': 4.99, 'ingredients': ['bread', 'tomatoes', 'onion', 'basil']}
            },
            'Main Courses': {
                'Steak': {'price': 15.99, 'ingredients': ['beef', 'salt', 'pepper']},
                'Salmon': {'price': 12.99, 'ingredients': ['salmon', 'lemon', 'dill']}
            },
            'Desserts': {
                'Ice Cream': {'price': 4.99, 'ingredients': ['milk', 'sugar', 'flavoring']},
                'Cake': {'price': 4.99, 'ingredients': ['flour', 'sugar', 'eggs']}
            }
        }

        # GUI Layout
        self.setup_widgets()

    def setup_widgets(self):
        # Button for adding a new menu item
        ttk.Button(self.master, text="Add New Dish", command=self.add_dish).pack(pady=10)

        # Button for updating an existing menu item
        ttk.Button(self.master, text="Update Dish", command=self.update_dish).pack(pady=10)

        # Display area for menu items
        self.text_display = tk.Text(self.master, height=15, width=50)
        self.text_display.pack(pady=20)

        # Initially display the current menu
        self.display_menu()

    def add_dish(self):
        category = simpledialog.askstring("Add Dish", "Enter the category:")
        dish_name = simpledialog.askstring("Add Dish", "Enter the dish name:")
        price = simpledialog.askfloat("Add Dish", "Enter the price:")
        ingredients = simpledialog.askstring("Add Dish", "Enter ingredients (comma-separated):")
        ingredients_list = ingredients.split(',')
```

```python
        self.add_menu_item(category, dish_name, price, ingredients_list)
        self.display_menu()

    def update_dish(self):
        category = simpledialog.askstring("Update Dish", "Enter the category:")
        dish_name = simpledialog.askstring("Update Dish", "Enter the dish name:")
        new_price = simpledialog.askfloat("Update Dish", "Enter the new price:")
        new_ingredients = simpledialog.askstring("Update Dish", "Enter new ingredients (comma-separated):")
        new_ingredients_list = new_ingredients.split(',') if new_ingredients else None

        self.update_menu_item(category, dish_name, new_price, new_ingredients_list)
        self.display_menu()

    def display_menu(self):
        self.text_display.delete('1.0', tk.END)
        for category, dishes in self.menu.items():
            self.text_display.insert(tk.END, f"{category}:\n")
            for dish, details in dishes.items():
                self.text_display.insert(tk.END, f"  {dish}: ${details['price']} - Ingredients: {', '.join(details['ingredients'])}\n")
            self.text_display.insert(tk.END, "\n")

    def add_menu_item(self, category, dish_name, price, ingredients):
        if category not in self.menu:
            self.menu[category] = {}
        self.menu[category][dish_name] = {'price': price, 'ingredients': ingredients}
        messagebox.showinfo("Success", f"Added {dish_name} to {category}.")

    def update_menu_item(self, category, dish_name, new_price, new_ingredients):
        if category in self.menu and dish_name in self.menu[category]:
            if new_price is not None:
                self.menu[category][dish_name]['price'] = new_price
            if new_ingredients is not None:
                self.menu[category][dish_name]['ingredients'] = new_ingredients
            messagebox.showinfo("Success", f"Updated {dish_name} in {category}.")
        else:
            messagebox.showerror("Error", "Dish not found.")

if __name__ == "__main__":
    root = tk.Tk()
    app = MenuManager(root)
    root.mainloop()
```

Explanation of the Code

1. Initialization (__init__):
   - The main window (master) is set up with a title and size.

- The restaurant's menu is stored in a dictionary.
2. Widget Setup (setup_widgets):
   This method configures the GUI layout, adding buttons for adding and updating dishes and a text display area for showing the menu.
3. Adding and Updating Dishes:
   add_dish() and update_dish() provide interfaces for user input via dialogues (simpledialog). They call respective functions to add or update dishes in the menu.
4. Display Menu (display_menu):
   Refreshes the text display area to show the current menu, formatting each category and its dishes neatly.
5. Interaction and Feedback:
   Uses message boxes (messagebox) to confirm successful operations or to report errors when a dish cannot be found for updates.

This application effectively demonstrates how a GUI can be used for dynamic data management, in this case, updating a restaurant's menu, allowing staff to keep the menu offerings current and accurate.

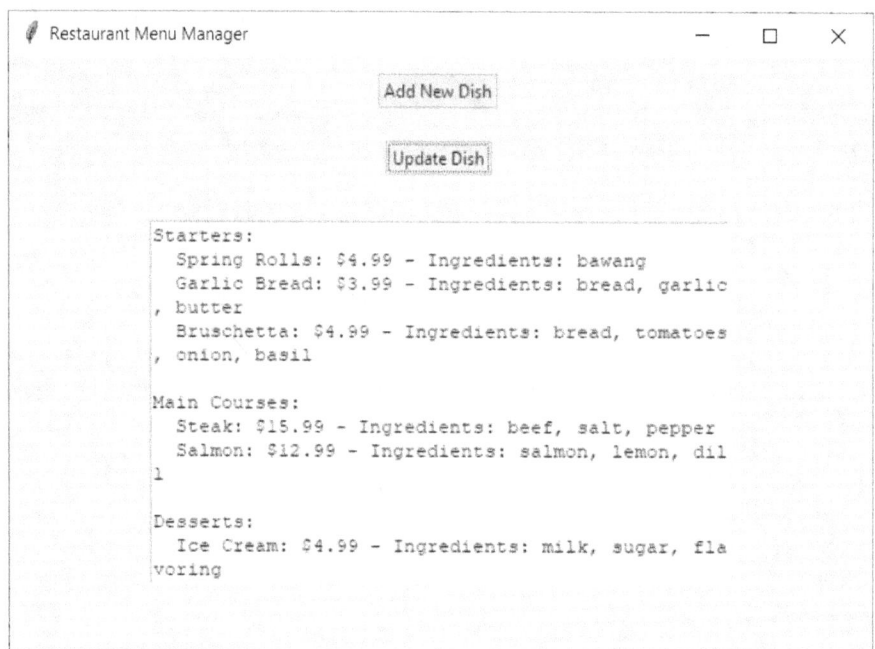

Example 1.7

E-commerce Shopping Cart System

In real-world applications, the ability to dynamically manage and remove elements from a dictionary can be critical, particularly in scenarios involving inventory management, user data handling, or session management. Here's a practical example where removing elements from a dictionary is essential: an e-commerce shopping cart system.

Scenario

Consider an online shopping platform where users can add items to their shopping cart, update quantities, or remove items entirely if they decide not to purchase them. The shopping cart for each user is managed using a dictionary where the product ID is the key, and a nested dictionary contains the product name, price, and quantity.

System Setup

1. Initial Shopping Cart Setup:

The shopping cart is represented as a dictionary. Each key is a product ID, and the value is another dictionary containing details about the product, such as name, price, and quantity.

```
shopping_cart = {
    101: {'name': 'Wireless Mouse', 'price': 25.99, 'quantity': 2},
    102: {'name': 'Keyboard', 'price': 45.50, 'quantity': 1},
    103: {'name': 'USB-C Charging Cable', 'price': 10.95, 'quantity': 3}
}
```

2. Removing an Item from the Cart:

A function to remove an item from the shopping cart by its product ID. If the product ID is found in the dictionary, it is removed.

```
def remove_item_from_cart(product_id):
    if product_id in shopping_cart:
        removed_item = shopping_cart.pop(product_id)
        print(f"Removed {removed_item['name']} from your cart.")
    else:
        print("Product not found in the cart.")
```

3. Interacting with the Shopping Cart:

Demonstrate removing an item and attempting to remove a non-existent item.

```
# Remove the Keyboard from the cart
```

```
remove_item_from_cart(102)   # Output: Removed Keyboard from your cart.

# Try to remove a non-existent item
remove_item_from_cart(999)   # Output: Product not found in the cart.
```

4. Printing the Current Cart Status:
A function to display the current contents of the cart.

```
def print_cart_contents():
    if shopping_cart:
        print("Your Shopping Cart:")
        for id, details in shopping_cart.items():
            print(f"Product ID {id}: {details['name']} - {details['quantity']} x ${details['price']}")
    else:
        print("Your cart is empty.")

print_cart_contents()   # Output the current state of the cart
```

Explanation
- Dynamic Dictionary Manipulation: The shopping cart uses a dictionary for fast access to items, adding, updating, or removing as needed by the user.
- Removing Items: The remove_item_from_cart function checks if the product ID exists in the dictionary and uses pop to remove it, which also returns the removed item's details.
- Feedback and Output: Upon removal, the user is informed of the action taken. If the product isn't found, a different message is displayed.

Benefits of Using a Dictionary in This Example
- Efficiency: Dictionaries provide an efficient way of storing and manipulating data with average time complexity of O(1) for lookups, insertions, and deletions.
- Flexibility: Items can be added or removed dynamically based on user interactions, which is ideal for scenarios like an online shopping cart where changes are frequent.
- Clarity: The structure of dictionaries allows for clear and logical representation of data, where each product ID directly maps to its details, making the code easier to understand and manage.

This example illustrates the practical application of dictionaries in handling dynamic datasets in e-commerce platforms, making them a powerful tool in backend systems for managing user-specific data like shopping carts.

Example 1.8
GUI Tkinter for E-commerce Shopping Cart System
To create a graphical user interface (GUI) in Tkinter that allows users to interact with the shopping cart, such as viewing, adding, and removing items dynamically, we'll develop a Python class-based application. This GUI will make the shopping experience more interactive and user-friendly.

Step 1: Define the GUI Class for the Shopping Cart
We'll start by setting up the main class, which will handle initializing the main window and manage interactions with the shopping cart data.

```python
import tkinter as tk
from tkinter import ttk, messagebox, simpledialog

class ShoppingCartApp:
    def __init__(self, master):
        self.master = master
        self.master.title("Shopping Cart Manager")
        self.master.geometry("400x300")

        # Initialize the shopping cart
        self.shopping_cart = {
            101: {'name': 'Wireless Mouse', 'price': 25.99, 'quantity': 2},
            102: {'name': 'Keyboard', 'price': 45.50, 'quantity': 1},
            103: {'name': 'USB-C Charging Cable', 'price': 10.95, 'quantity': 3}
        }

        # Setting up the user interface
        self.setup_widgets()

    def setup_widgets(self):
        # Label to display the shopping cart contents
        self.label = ttk.Label(self.master, text="Shopping Cart Contents", font=('Arial', 16))
        self.label.pack(pady=10)

        # Listbox to display cart items
        self.listbox = tk.Listbox(self.master, width=50, height=10)
        self.listbox.pack(pady=5)
```

```python
        # Buttons to interact with the shopping cart
        ttk.Button(self.master, text="Remove Item", command=self.remove_item).pack(pady=5)
        ttk.Button(self.master, text="Show Cart", command=self.print_cart_contents).pack(pady=5)

        # Initially display cart contents
        self.print_cart_contents()

    def remove_item(self):
        # Get the selected item's index
        selected_index = self.listbox.curselection()
        if not selected_index:
            messagebox.showerror("Error", "No item selected")
            return
        item_key = list(self.shopping_cart.keys())[selected_index[0]]
        removed_item = self.shopping_cart.pop(item_key)
        messagebox.showinfo("Item Removed", f"Removed {removed_item['name']} from your cart.")
        self.print_cart_contents()

    def print_cart_contents(self):
        self.listbox.delete(0, tk.END)  # Clear the listbox first
        if self.shopping_cart:
            for id, details in self.shopping_cart.items():
                self.listbox.insert(tk.END, f"Product ID {id}: {details['name']} - {details['quantity']} x ${details['price']}")
        else:
            self.listbox.insert(tk.END, "Your cart is empty.")

if __name__ == "__main__":
    root = tk.Tk()
    app = ShoppingCartApp(root)
    root.mainloop()
```

Explanation of the Code

1. Class Definition (ShoppingCartApp):
   The class initializes the main window and sets up the GUI components to interact with the shopping cart data.
2. setup_widgets Method:
   This method configures the GUI layout, adding a label for the title, a listbox for displaying cart items, and buttons for removing items and showing the cart contents.
3. Removing Items from Cart (remove_item):

This function identifies the selected item in the listbox, retrieves the corresponding product ID from the shopping cart, and removes that item. It updates the listbox to reflect the changes.

4. Displaying Cart Contents (print_cart_contents):

Refreshes the listbox display to show the current items in the shopping cart or indicates if the cart is empty.

Features of the GUI
- Interactive List Display: Users can see all items in their shopping cart in a scrollable list, making it easy to review what they have added.
- Dynamic Updates: The GUI updates in real-time as items are removed, ensuring the display always matches the current state of the shopping cart.
- User Feedback: The application uses message boxes to provide immediate feedback on actions, such as confirming the removal of an item or alerting when no item is selected.

This application demonstrates a practical implementation of a shopping cart system with a graphical user interface, making it easier and more intuitive for users to manage their shopping experience.

Example 1.9
Retail Inventory Management System

In the real world, checking whether a key exists in a dictionary is a common task across many applications, from web development to data analysis. Let's consider a real-world scenario involving inventory management in a retail setting, which showcases how checking for a key in a dictionary can be effectively utilized.

Scenario

Imagine you're managing the inventory for a retail store that sells a variety of products. Each product is identified by a unique SKU (Stock Keeping Unit). The inventory is managed using a Python dictionary where the SKU is the key, and the value is another dictionary containing details about the product such as name, price, and stock level.

System Setup

1. Initial Inventory Setup:

Here is an example dictionary setup for managing inventory:

```
inventory = {
    "SKU123": {"name": "T-shirt", "price": 19.99, "stock": 120},
    "SKU124": {"name": "Jeans", "price": 39.99, "stock": 60},
    "SKU125": {"name": "Socks", "price": 4.99, "stock": 200}
}
```

2. Checking for Product Availability:

A function to check if a product exists in the inventory by its SKU.

```
def check_product_availability(sku):
    if sku in inventory:
        product = inventory[sku]
        return f"Product: {product['name']}, Price: ${product['price']}, Stock: {product['stock']}"
    else:
        return "Product not found."
```

3. Use Case:

Let's use this function to check the availability of a few products.

```
# Check if a specific product SKU exists in the inventory
print(check_product_availability("SKU123"))  # Output: Product: T-shirt, Price: $19.99, Stock: 120
print(check_product_availability("SKU999"))  # Output: Product not found.
```

Explanation
- Checking Existence of Key: The function check_product_availability uses the in keyword to check if the given SKU exists in the inventory dictionary. This operation is fast and efficient, making it ideal for real-time inventory checks in a retail environment.
- Feedback: The function provides immediate feedback about the product's availability, price, and stock level if found, or informs the user if the product is not available.

Benefits of Using Dictionaries for This Task
- Efficiency: Dictionaries in Python are implemented as hash tables. The average time complexity for checking if a key exists, accessing a value, or inserting an item is O(1), making dictionaries extremely efficient for these operations.
- Readability: Using a dictionary makes the code more readable and straightforward, as accessing elements and checking for keys are clear and concise operations.
- Scalability: Dictionaries handle large datasets well, so this method scales effectively as inventory grows.

This example illustrates a common use case in many business applications where dictionaries provide a simple and efficient way to manage and query data dynamically based on unique identifiers. Such applications are prevalent in retail, warehousing, and any other domain where itemized data management is crucial.

Example 1.10
GUI Tkinter for Retail Inventory Management System

To create a rich graphical user interface (GUI) using Tkinter that allows users to interact with the inventory data, we can develop a Python class-based application that integrates the checking of product availability. This GUI will make it easier for users, such as store employees, to quickly check if a product is available without needing to manually search through data lists or databases.

Step 1: Define the GUI Class for Inventory Management
We'll start by setting up the main class for our GUI, which will manage initializing the main window and controlling interactions with the inventory data.

```python
import tkinter as tk
from tkinter import ttk, messagebox, simpledialog

class InventoryApp:
    def __init__(self, master):
        self.master = master
        self.master.title("Inventory Management System")
        self.master.geometry("400x300")

        # Initialize the inventory
        self.inventory = {
            "SKU123": {"name": "T-shirt", "price": 19.99, "stock": 120},
            "SKU124": {"name": "Jeans", "price": 39.99, "stock": 60},
            "SKU125": {"name": "Socks", "price": 4.99, "stock": 200}
        }

        # GUI Layout
        self.setup_widgets()

    def setup_widgets(self):
        # Label for instructions
        ttk.Label(self.master, text="Enter SKU to check availability:", font=('Arial', 14)).pack(pady=10)

        # Entry field for SKU input
        self.sku_entry = ttk.Entry(self.master, width=20, font=('Arial', 14))
        self.sku_entry.pack(pady=10)

        # Button to check product availability
        ttk.Button(self.master, text="Check Availability", command=self.check_availability).pack(pady=10)

        # Label for displaying results
        self.result_label = ttk.Label(self.master, text="", font=('Arial', 14))
        self.result_label.pack(pady=20)

    def check_availability(self):
        sku = self.sku_entry.get()
        result = self.check_product_availability(sku)
        self.result_label.config(text=result)

    def check_product_availability(self, sku):
        if sku in self.inventory:
            product = self.inventory[sku]
            return f"Product: {product['name']}, Price: ${product['price']}, Stock: {product['stock']}"
        else:
            return "Product not found."

if __name__ == "__main__":
```

```
root = tk.Tk()
app = InventoryApp(root)
root.mainloop()
```

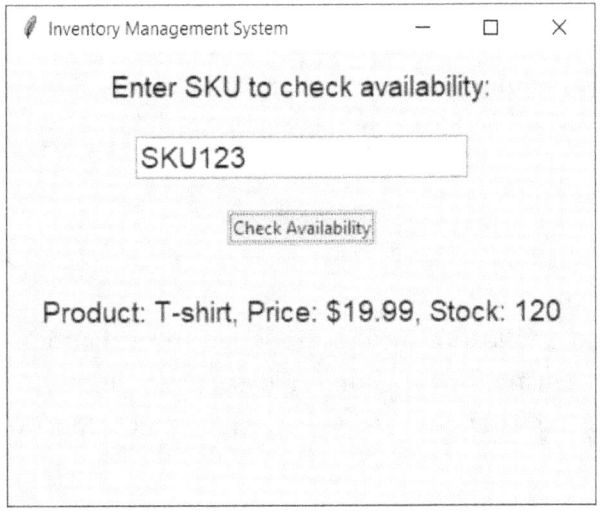

Explanation of the Code
1. Class Definition (InventoryApp):
   Initializes the main window and sets up the GUI components to interact with the inventory data.
2. setup_widgets Method:
   Configures the GUI layout, adding an entry field for users to enter a SKU, a button to trigger the availability check, and a label to display results.
3. Checking Product Availability (check_availability):
   - Retrieves the SKU from the entry widget and calls check_product_availability to check if the SKU exists in the inventory.
   - Updates the GUI with the result by setting the text of result_label.
4. Interaction and Feedback:
   Provides a clear interface for inputting SKUs and displays whether the product is available directly in the GUI.

Features of the GUI
- User Input and Interaction: The GUI is designed to be user-friendly, with clear labels and an easy-to-use input field for checking product availability.
- Dynamic Feedback: Immediately updates the GUI to show whether a product is available, enhancing the user experience.

- Simplicity and Effectiveness: The application is straightforward but effectively demonstrates how a GUI can simplify tasks such as inventory checks in real-world settings.

This GUI application provides an intuitive way for store employees or managers to quickly check the availability of items in their inventory, improving efficiency and usability compared to manual checks or command-line queries.

Example 1.11
Event Registration System

A practical real-world application where the length of a dictionary is crucial involves managing an event registration system. This scenario utilizes dictionary operations extensively to handle registrations, check capacities, and report on current enrollment statuses.

Scenario Overview

Imagine you are organizing a series of workshops and seminars. Each event has a limited capacity, and you want to track how many participants have registered for each event to ensure it does not become overbooked. You also need to provide quick updates on how many events are currently on offer and how many are fully booked.

System Setup

1. Event Setup:

You will use a dictionary where each key is an event ID and the value is another dictionary containing details about the event, such as the event name, maximum participants, and a list of registered participants.

```
events = {
    1: {'name': "Python Workshop", 'max_participants': 30, 'participants': ['Alice', 'Bob', 'Charlie']},
    2: {'name': "Data Science Seminar", 'max_participants': 25, 'participants': ['David']},
    3: {'name': "Machine Learning Panel", 'max_participants': 50, 'participants': []}
}
```

2. Checking Total Events:

To get an overview of how many events are currently active, you simply check the length of the events dictionary.

```
def get_total_events():
    return len(events)

# Example Usage
total_events = get_total_events()
print(f"There are currently {total_events} events available for registration.")
```

3. Checking for Full Events:

You may also need to find out how many events have already reached their capacity to either announce they are full or to close registration.

```
def count_full_events():
    full_count = 0
    for event_id, details in events.items():
        if len(details['participants']) >= details['max_participants']:
            full_count += 1
    return full_count

# Example Usage
full_events = count_full_events()
print(f"There are {full_events} events that are fully booked.")
```

Explanation

- Length of Dictionary: Using len(events) provides the total count of events managed in the system. This is a straightforward and efficient way to determine how many events are being tracked without iterating through all data.
- Calculating Full Events: The function count_full_events iterates through each event and checks if the length of the participants list is greater than or equal to max_participants. This use case highlights how the length of a dictionary (or its sub-elements) is essential for capacity management.

Benefits of Using Dictionaries

- Efficient Data Access: Dictionaries allow fast access to any entry by its key, making operations like checking participant lists or updating them very efficient.
- Flexibility: The dictionary structure can easily be expanded, for example, to include more detailed event descriptions or multiple session times per event without altering how counts are performed.
- Simplicity: Utilizing Python dictionaries simplifies data manipulation, making the code easier to maintain and understand compared to other data structures like lists of lists or more complex database systems for smaller scale requirements.

This example demonstrates how dictionaries are particularly useful in managing structured data where elements are accessed frequently and need to be updated dynamically, typical in applications like event registration platforms.

Example 1.12
GUI Tkinter for Event Registration System
To create a rich graphical user interface (GUI) in Tkinter that allows users to interact with an event management system, we'll develop a Python class-based application. This application will allow users to view events, check the total number of events, and see how many events are fully booked.

Step 1: Define the GUI Class for Event Management
The main class for our GUI will manage initializing the main window and provide interaction methods to manipulate and view event data.

```python
import tkinter as tk
from tkinter import ttk

class EventManagerApp:
    def __init__(self, master):
        self.master = master
        self.master.title("Event Manager")
        self.master.geometry("600x400")
        
        # Event data
        self.events = {
            1: {'name': "Python Workshop", 'max_participants': 30, 'participants': ['Alice', 'Bob', 'Charlie']},
            2: {'name': "Data Science Seminar", 'max_participants': 25, 'participants': ['David']},
            3: {'name': "Machine Learning Panel", 'max_participants': 50, 'participants': []}
        }
        
        # GUI Setup
        self.setup_widgets()

    def setup_widgets(self):
        # Create a Treeview to display the event information
        self.tree = ttk.Treeview(self.master, columns=('Event ID', 'Event Name', 'Max Participants', 'Current Participants'), show='headings')
        self.tree.heading('Event ID', text='Event ID')
        self.tree.heading('Event Name', text='Event Name')
```

```
            self.tree.heading('Max Participants', text='Max Participants')
            self.tree.heading('Current Participants', text='Current Participants')
            self.tree.pack(fill=tk.BOTH, expand=True)

            # Buttons for actions
            ttk.Button(self.master,         text="Show         Total         Events",
command=self.show_total_events).pack(pady=5)
            ttk.Button(self.master,         text="Show         Full          Events",
command=self.show_full_events).pack(pady=5)

            # Initially populate the Treeview
            self.populate_treeview()

    def populate_treeview(self):
        for event_id, details in self.events.items():
            self.tree.insert('',    tk.END,    values=(event_id,    details['name'],
details['max_participants'], len(details['participants'])))

    def show_total_events(self):
        total = len(self.events)
        tk.messagebox.showinfo("Total Events", f"There are currently {total} events
available for registration.")

    def show_full_events(self):
        full_count = 0
        for details in self.events.values():
            if len(details['participants']) >= details['max_participants']:
                full_count += 1
        tk.messagebox.showinfo("Full Events", f"There are {full_count} events that are
fully booked.")

if __name__ == "__main__":
    root = tk.Tk()
    app = EventManagerApp(root)
    root.mainloop()
```

Explanation of the Code
1. Class Definition (EventManagerApp):
   Initializes the main window and sets up GUI components to interact with the event data. The class uses a Treeview for displaying event details in a table-like format.
2. setup_widgets Method:
   Configures the GUI layout, adding a Treeview to display the events and buttons to retrieve total and full events. Each event's details, including the current number of participants, are shown.
3. Adding Events to Treeview:

The populate_treeview() method inserts each event into the Treeview with its ID, name, maximum participants, and the current number of participants.

4. Interactions for Event Counting:
show_total_events() and show_full_events() methods compute and display the total number of events and the number of fully booked events using message boxes for user-friendly notifications.

Features of the GUI

- Interactive Display: Users can visually scan all events, their capacities, and participant counts.
- Dynamic Feedback: The GUI provides instant feedback on the total number of events and which are fully booked, enhancing user interaction.
- Ease of Use: The GUI's layout and functionality are straightforward, making it easy for users to manage and view event statuses.

This GUI application effectively demonstrates how a graphical interface can be utilized for managing events, providing a simple yet powerful tool for event organizers to monitor registrations and capacities.

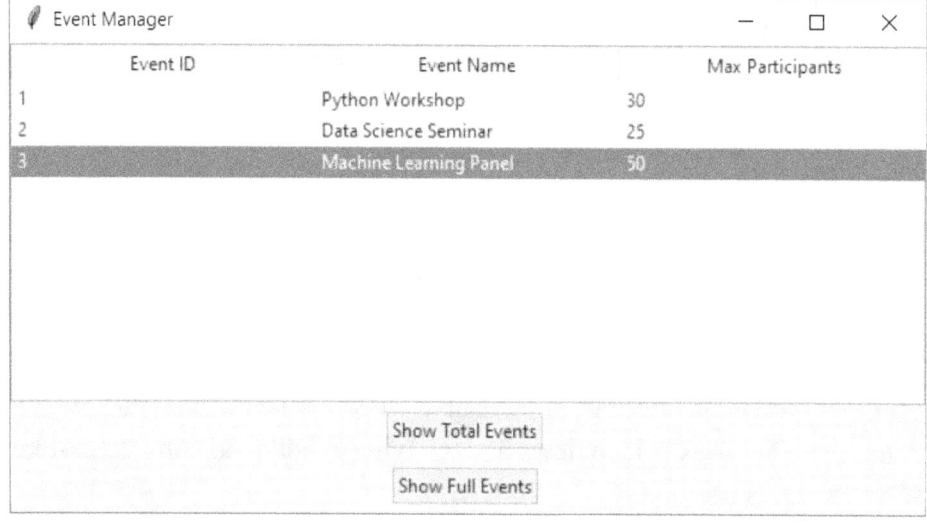

Example 1.13
Retail Sales Report Generation
In real-world applications, iterating through dictionaries is a common task when you need to process or manipulate data stored in key-value pairs. A practical example of this is generating reports from sales data in a retail business environment.

Scenario
Imagine you are running a retail store, and you have a dictionary that records the sales data for different products. Each key in the dictionary represents a product, and the value is another dictionary that contains details about the sales of that product, such as the total units sold and total revenue generated.

System Setup
1. Initial Sales Data Setup:
Here's how the sales data might be structured using a Python dictionary:

```python
sales_data = {
    'Apples': {'units_sold': 120, 'revenue': 360},
    'Bananas': {'units_sold': 100, 'revenue': 250},
    'Cherries': {'units_sold': 75, 'revenue': 300}
}
```

2. Iterating Through Sales Data:
A function to calculate the total revenue and total units sold across all products can be created. This function will iterate through each item in the dictionary to sum up these values.

```python
def calculate_totals(sales_dict):
    total_units = 0
    total_revenue = 0
    for product, details in sales_dict.items():
        total_units += details['units_sold']
        total_revenue += details['revenue']
    return total_units, total_revenue

# Example Usage
total_units_sold, total_revenue_generated = calculate_totals(sales_data)
print(f"Total    units    sold:    {total_units_sold},    Total    revenue: ${total_revenue_generated}")
```

3. Generating Detailed Sales Report:
Another function could iterate through the dictionary to print a detailed report for each product.

```
def generate_sales_report(sales_dict):
    print("Sales Report:")
    for product, details in sales_dict.items():
        print(f"{product}:    Units    Sold:    {details['units_sold']},    Revenue: ${details['revenue']}")

# Example Usage
generate_sales_report(sales_data)
```

Explanation

- Iterating Through Dictionary: In calculate_totals, the items() method of the dictionary is used to iterate over each key-value pair. This is useful for accessing both the key (product name) and the value (sales details).
- Summing Up Data: During iteration, the function accumulates total units and total revenue, demonstrating how to aggregate data from dictionaries.
- Detailed Report Generation: The generate_sales_report function iterates over each entry in the dictionary to output detailed sales information for each product, which is useful for financial reporting or stock management.

Benefits of Using Dictionaries for This Task

- Efficient Data Access and Manipulation: Dictionaries provide O(1) average time complexity for accessing elements, which is optimal for frequently accessed data.
- Flexibility in Data Structure: The nested dictionary structure allows complex data storage and is straightforward to manipulate as part of regular business operations, such as sales tracking and reporting.
- Readability and Maintainability: Using dictionaries and their built-in methods to iterate data makes the code more readable and easier to maintain or extend, such as adding more product details or sales metrics.

This example illustrates the practical utility of dictionaries in handling structured data efficiently, especially in scenarios where data needs to be regularly accessed and aggregated, such as in generating sales reports in retail environments.

Example 1.14
GUI Tkinter for Retail Sales Report Generation
To develop a graphical user interface (GUI) using Tkinter for displaying and interacting with the sales data described, we'll build a Python class-based application. This GUI will enable users to view sales reports directly through the interface and dynamically calculate totals.

Step 1: Define the GUI Class for Sales Data Interaction
We'll set up the main class for our GUI, managing the initialization of the main window and providing methods for displaying sales data and calculating totals.

```python
import tkinter as tk
from tkinter import ttk

class SalesDataApp:
    def __init__(self, master):
        self.master = master
        self.master.title("Sales Data Manager")
        self.master.geometry("400x300")

        self.sales_data = {
            'Apples': {'units_sold': 120, 'revenue': 360},
            'Bananas': {'units_sold': 100, 'revenue': 250},
            'Cherries': {'units_sold': 75, 'revenue': 300}
        }

        # Setup GUI components
        self.setup_widgets()

    def setup_widgets(self):
        # Button to show total sales and revenue
        ttk.Button(self.master, text="Show Totals", command=self.display_totals).pack(pady=10)

        # Button to generate and display sales report
        ttk.Button(self.master, text="Generate Sales Report", command=self.display_sales_report).pack(pady=10)

        # Text box for displaying results
        self.text_display = tk.Text(self.master, height=10, width=50)
        self.text_display.pack(pady=20)

    def display_totals(self):
        total_units, total_revenue = self.calculate_totals(self.sales_data)
        message = f"Total units sold: {total_units}, Total revenue: ${total_revenue}"
        self.text_display.delete('1.0', tk.END)  # Clear the text box
```

```
        self.text_display.insert(tk.END, message)

    def display_sales_report(self):
        report = "Sales Report:\n"
        for product, details in self.sales_data.items():
            report += f"{product}: Units Sold: {details['units_sold']}, Revenue: ${details['revenue']}\n"
        self.text_display.delete('1.0', tk.END)  # Clear the text box
        self.text_display.insert(tk.END, report)

    def calculate_totals(self, sales_dict):
        total_units = 0
        total_revenue = 0
        for product, details in sales_dict.items():
            total_units += details['units_sold']
            total_revenue += details['revenue']
        return total_units, total_revenue

if __name__ == "__main__":
    root = tk.Tk()
    app = SalesDataApp(root)
    root.mainloop()
```

Explanation of the Code

1. Class Definition (SalesDataApp):

    Initializes the main window (master) and sets up GUI components for interacting with sales data. The class manages displaying sales data and calculating totals directly in the GUI.

2. Widget Setup (setup_widgets):

    Configures the GUI layout, adding buttons for showing total sales data and generating a sales report. A text display area (Text) is used for outputting information to the user.

3. Displaying Totals and Reports:
    - display_totals calculates and shows the total units sold and total revenue by calling calculate_totals, which iterates through the sales_data dictionary to sum values.
    - display_sales_report generates a detailed sales report by iterating through each item in sales_data and formatting it into a readable string that is displayed in the text widget.

Features of the GUI
- Interactive Display: Users can interactively view total sales data and detailed sales reports with the click of a button.
- Dynamic Updates: The GUI updates the displayed information in real-time based on user requests, which makes it very responsive and user-friendly.
- Clear Feedback: The application uses a large text display area to provide clear, easy-to-read feedback directly in the GUI.

This GUI application provides a practical demonstration of how a graphical user interface can enhance data interaction, particularly for tasks like viewing and calculating sales data in a retail or business environment. This setup makes the process more intuitive and accessible compared to command-line or script-based interactions.

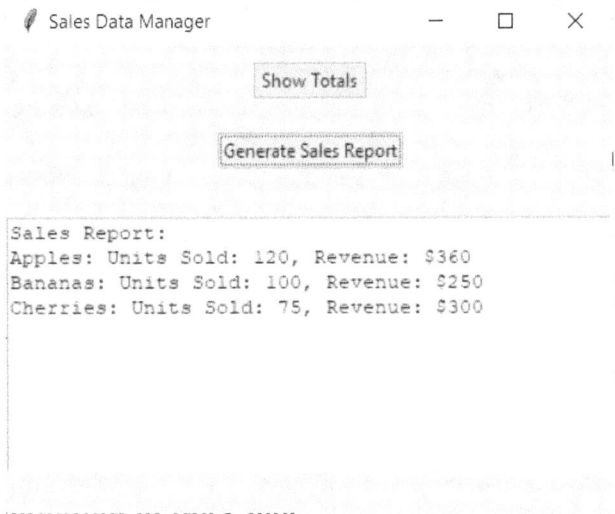

Example 1.15
Electronics Store Inventory System
Let's consider a simple real-world example demonstrating the basic operations of a dictionary in Python by managing an inventory system for a small electronics store. This example will illustrate how to add items, update stock quantities, remove items, and access details about the stock.

We'll create a dictionary to manage the inventory of products, which includes operations such as adding new products, updating the stock count, checking stock, removing products from inventory, and listing all products.

Setup the Basic Structure

Here's how we might set up our inventory system using a dictionary:

```
# Initial Inventory Setup
inventory = {
    "laptop": {"brand": "Dell", "quantity": 10, "price": 800},
    "smartphone": {"brand": "Apple", "quantity": 15, "price": 999},
    "tablet": {"brand": "Samsung", "quantity": 20, "price": 600}
}

# Function to add a new product to the inventory
def add_product(product_name, brand, quantity, price):
    if product_name in inventory:
        print(f"{product_name} already exists in the inventory.")
    else:
        inventory[product_name] = {"brand": brand, "quantity": quantity, "price": price}
        print(f"Added {quantity} units of {brand} {product_name} at ${price} each.")

# Function to update existing product quantity
def update_quantity(product_name, quantity):
    if product_name in inventory:
        inventory[product_name]["quantity"] += quantity
        print(f"Updated {product_name} stock by {quantity}. Total now: {inventory[product_name]['quantity']}")
    else:
        print(f"{product_name} does not exist in inventory.")

# Function to check the stock of a product
def check_stock(product_name):
    if product_name in inventory:
        product_details = inventory[product_name]
        print(f"Stock for {product_name}: {product_details['quantity']} units.")
    else:
        print(f"{product_name} not found in inventory.")

# Function to remove a product from the inventory
def remove_product(product_name):
```

```
    if product_name in inventory:
        del inventory[product_name]
        print(f"Removed {product_name} from inventory.")
    else:
        print(f"{product_name} not found in inventory.")

# Function to list all products in the inventory
def list_products():
    print("Current Inventory:")
    for product, details in inventory.items():
        print(f"{product}: {details['quantity']} units, ${details['price']} each, Brand: {details['brand']}")

# Example Usage
add_product("headphones", "Sony", 30, 150)
update_quantity("tablet", 5)
check_stock("laptop")
remove_product("smartphone")
list_products()
```

Description

- Dictionary Structure: The inventory dictionary uses product names as keys and each key has a value of another dictionary containing brand, quantity, and price.
- Basic Operations:
- Adding Products: add_product() checks if the product exists and adds it if it does not.
- Updating Inventory: update_quantity() modifies the quantity of an existing product.
- Checking Stock: check_stock() displays the quantity available for a specified product.
- Removing Products: remove_product() deletes a product from the dictionary.
- Listing Inventory: list_products() iterates through the dictionary and prints out all the product details.

Conclusion

This example clearly demonstrates how to manage an electronic store's inventory using basic dictionary operations in Python. This system can easily be expanded with more features such as tracking sales, generating reports, or even integrating with a point-of-sale system for real-time inventory updates. The flexibility and straightforwardness of dictionaries make them ideal for such applications.

Example 1.16
GUI Tkinter for Electronics Store Inventory System
To create a robust GUI application using Tkinter and encapsulate the functionality within a class, let's develop an inventory management system that includes adding, updating, removing products, and listing inventory items.

Below are the steps to build this application, including class definitions, method implementations, and GUI component setup.

Step 1: Define the GUI Class for Inventory Management
We'll start by creating a class that encapsulates the inventory and its operations, along with GUI interactions.

```
import tkinter as tk
from tkinter import messagebox, simpledialog, ttk

class InventoryApp:
    def __init__(self, master):
        self.master = master
        self.master.title("Inventory Management System")
        self.master.geometry("500x300")

        self.inventory = {
            "laptop": {"brand": "Dell", "quantity": 10, "price": 800},
            "smartphone": {"brand": "Apple", "quantity": 15, "price": 999},
            "tablet": {"brand": "Samsung", "quantity": 20, "price": 600}
        }

        self.setup_ui()

    def setup_ui(self):
        # Setup buttons and labels
        ttk.Button(self.master, text="Add Product", command=self.gui_add_product).pack(pady=5)
        ttk.Button(self.master, text="Update Quantity", command=self.gui_update_quantity).pack(pady=5)
        ttk.Button(self.master, text="Remove Product", command=self.gui_remove_product).pack(pady=5)
        ttk.Button(self.master, text="Check Stock", command=self.gui_check_stock).pack(pady=5)
```

```python
        ttk.Button(self.master, text="List Products", command=self.gui_list_products).pack(pady=5)

        self.text_area = tk.Text(self.master, height=10, width=50)
        self.text_area.pack(pady=10)

    def add_product(self, product_name, brand, quantity, price):
        if product_name in self.inventory:
            messagebox.showinfo("Error", f"{product_name} already exists in the inventory.")
        else:
            self.inventory[product_name] = {"brand": brand, "quantity": quantity, "price": price}
            messagebox.showinfo("Success", f"Added {quantity} units of {brand} {product_name} at ${price} each.")
            self.gui_list_products()

    def update_quantity(self, product_name, quantity):
        if product_name in self.inventory:
            self.inventory[product_name]["quantity"] += quantity
            messagebox.showinfo("Success", f"Updated {product_name} stock by {quantity}. Total now: {self.inventory[product_name]['quantity']}")
        else:
            messagebox.showerror("Error", f"{product_name} does not exist in inventory.")

    def remove_product(self, product_name):
        if product_name in self.inventory:
            del self.inventory[product_name]
            messagebox.showinfo("Success", f"Removed {product_name} from inventory.")
            self.gui_list_products()
        else:
            messagebox.showerror("Error", f"{product_name} not found in inventory.")

    def check_stock(self, product_name):
        if product_name in self.inventory:
            product_details = self.inventory[product_name]
            messagebox.showinfo("Stock Check", f"Stock for {product_name}: {product_details['quantity']} units.")
        else:
            messagebox.showerror("Error", f"{product_name} not found in inventory.")

    def list_products(self):
        self.text_area.delete('1.0', tk.END)
        self.text_area.insert(tk.END, "Current Inventory:\n")
        for product, details in self.inventory.items():
            self.text_area.insert(tk.END, f"{product}: {details['quantity']} units, ${details['price']} each, Brand: {details['brand']}\n")

    # GUI wrappers for functions
```

```python
    def gui_add_product(self):
        product_name = simpledialog.askstring("Add Product", "Enter product name:")
        brand = simpledialog.askstring("Add Product", "Enter brand:")
        quantity = simpledialog.askinteger("Add Product", "Enter quantity:")
        price = simpledialog.askinteger("Add Product", "Enter price:")
        self.add_product(product_name, brand, quantity, price)

    def gui_update_quantity(self):
        product_name = simpledialog.askstring("Update Quantity", "Enter product name:")
        quantity = simpledialog.askinteger("Update Quantity", "Enter quantity to add (or subtract, e.g., -5):")
        self.update_quantity(product_name, quantity)

    def gui_remove_product(self):
        product_name = simpledialog.askstring("Remove Product", "Enter product name:")
        self.remove_product(product_name)

    def gui_check_stock(self):
        product_name = simpledialog.askstring("Check Stock", "Enter product name:")
        self.check_stock(product_name)

    def gui_list_products(self):
        self.list_products()

# Run the application
if __name__ == "__main__":
    root = tk.Tk()
    app = InventoryApp(root)
    root.mainloop()
```

Explanation

- Class Structure: InventoryApp initializes the main window and sets up the UI components such as buttons and a text area for displaying inventory details.
- Inventory Operations: Methods like add_product, update_quantity, remove_product, check_stock, and list_products manage the inventory based on user inputs and interactions.
- GUI Interaction: Dialogs (simpledialog) gather user inputs, and inventory operations are triggered through button clicks. Feedback is provided using message boxes (messagebox).
- Dynamic Inventory Display: The inventory is dynamically listed in the text area, updating in real-time as inventory changes are made.

This GUI application provides a comprehensive interface for managing an inventory system, making it intuitive and accessible for users to perform various inventory-related operations.

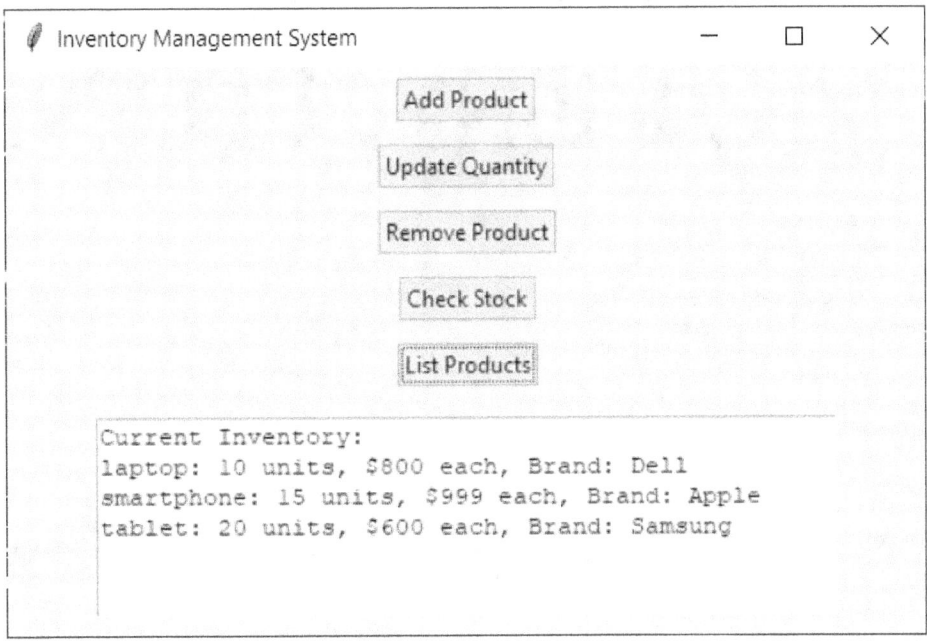

ADVANCED OPERATIONS

INTRODUCTION

Dictionary Comprehensions:

Similar to list comprehensions, dictionary comprehensions offer a concise way to create dictionaries.

```
{x: x**2 for x in (2, 4, 6)}   # {2: 4, 4: 16, 6: 36}
```

Merging Dictionaries:

As of Python 3.9, you can merge dictionaries using the | operator.

```
dict1 = {"a": 1, "b": 2}
dict2 = {"c": 3, "d": 4}
merged = dict1 | dict2
```

Copying:

Dictionaries can be copied using the copy() method.

```
new_dict = my_dict.copy()
```

Clearing:

Remove all items from the dictionary using clear().

```
my_dict.clear()
```

Using get():
The get() method returns the value for a key if it exists in the dictionary. If not, it returns None, or a specified default value.

```
email = my_dict.get("email", "No email provided")
```

Using setdefault():
This method returns the value of a key if it is in the dictionary; if not, it inserts the key with a specified value.

```
my_dict.setdefault("email", "default@example.com")
```

Dictionaries in Python are highly versatile and can be used in various applications like counting items, grouping data, and building complex data models. They are one of the core data structures and are extremely useful in many programming and data processing tasks.

Example 2.1
Sales Analysis System

Dictionary comprehensions in Python provide a concise way to create dictionaries. Let's explore a real-world example demonstrating dictionary comprehensions by setting up a system for analyzing a dataset of sales records. This example will involve creating dictionaries to categorize and summarize sales data, helping a business to quickly understand sales performance across different product categories.

Imagine a business that needs to summarize its sales data to understand the total sales per product and the average price per product sold. This dataset is initially stored as a list of tuples, each tuple containing the product name, the number sold, and the price at which each unit was sold.

Setup the Basic Dataset and Operations
Here's how we could set up our sales analysis using dictionary comprehensions:

```
# Sample data: a list of tuples (product, units sold, price per unit)
sales_data = [
```

```python
        ("laptop", 5, 1200),
        ("laptop", 3, 1250),
        ("smartphone", 10, 700),
        ("smartphone", 5, 750),
        ("tablet", 11, 400),
        ("tablet", 6, 420)
]

# Using dictionary comprehension to calculate total sales per product
total_sales = {product: sum(units * price for p, units, price in sales_data if p == product)
                for product, _, _ in sales_data}

# Using dictionary comprehension to calculate total units sold per product
total_units = {product: sum(units for p, units, _ in sales_data if p == product)
                for product, _, _ in sales_data}

# Using dictionary comprehension to calculate average price per product
average_price = {product: total_sales[product] / total_units[product] for product in total_units}

# Printing the results
print("Total Sales per Product:")
for product, total in total_sales.items():
    print(f"{product}: ${total}")

print("\nAverage Price per Product:")
for product, avg in average_price.items():
    print(f"{product}: ${avg:.2f}")

# Output:
# Total Sales per Product:
# laptop: $18750
# smartphone: $11250
# tablet: $7260
#
# Average Price per Product:
# laptop: $1215.38
# smartphone: $718.75
# tablet: $412.86
```

Explanation

- Total Sales per Product: This dictionary is generated using a comprehension that iterates through the sales_data list and calculates the sum of sales for each product (product sales are calculated by multiplying units sold by price per unit).
- Total Units Sold per Product: Another dictionary is formed by iterating through sales_data and summing up the units sold for each product.
- Average Price per Product: The average price per product is calculated using the results of the first two dictionaries. The formula divides the total sales by the total units sold for each product. This is also done using a dictionary comprehension.

Benefits of Dictionary Comprehensions
- Conciseness and Readability: The comprehensions allow the logic to be expressed very compactly while still being readable.
- Direct Mapping: Comprehensions provide a direct way of transforming data into the desired dictionary format, making data manipulation tasks straightforward.
- Performance: Dictionary comprehensions are generally faster for creating dictionaries from iterables than using a loop and appending to a dictionary because they are optimized for this specific task.

Conclusion
This example illustrates how dictionary comprehensions can be used effectively in real-world applications to perform data aggregation and transformation tasks, such as summarizing and analyzing sales data. By leveraging dictionary comprehensions, developers can write cleaner, more efficient, and more Pythonic code, especially useful in data analysis and processing tasks.

Example 2.2
GUI Tkinter for Sales Analysis System
To create a rich GUI in Tkinter using the provided sales data and analysis, we'll develop a class-based application that displays the aggregated sales data in a user-friendly interface. This application will not only allow users to view summarized sales data but also dynamically interact with it, such as filtering by product type.

Step 1: Setup the Basic Structure of the Application
First, we initialize the main window and set up the basic class structure for the Tkinter GUI.

```python
import tkinter as tk
from tkinter import ttk

class SalesApp:
    def __init__(self, master):
        self.master = master
        self.master.title("Sales Analysis Dashboard")
        self.master.geometry("400x300")

        self.setup_widgets()

    def setup_widgets(self):
        # Setup the layout - labels and treeview for displaying data
        self.tree = ttk.Treeview(self.master, columns=('Product', 'Total Sales', 'Average Price'), show='headings')
        self.tree.heading('Product', text='Product')
        self.tree.heading('Total Sales', text='Total Sales')
        self.tree.heading('Average Price', text='Average Price')
        self.tree.pack(fill=tk.BOTH, expand=True)

        self.populate_data()

    def populate_data(self):
        # Sample data
        sales_data = [
            ("laptop", 5, 1200),
            ("laptop", 3, 1250),
            ("smartphone", 10, 700),
            ("smartphone", 5, 750),
            ("tablet", 11, 400),
            ("tablet", 6, 420)
        ]

        # Aggregating data
        total_sales = {product: sum(units * price for p, units, price in sales_data if p == product)
                       for product, _, _ in sales_data}
        total_units = {product: sum(units for p, units, _ in sales_data if p == product)
                       for product, _, _ in sales_data}
        average_price = {product: total_sales[product] / total_units[product] for product in total_units}

        # Inserting data into the Treeview
        for product in total_sales:
            self.tree.insert('', tk.END, values=(product, f"${total_sales[product]:,.2f}", f"${average_price[product]:.2f}"))

# Create the application
root = tk.Tk()
```

```
app = SalesApp(root)
root.mainloop()
```

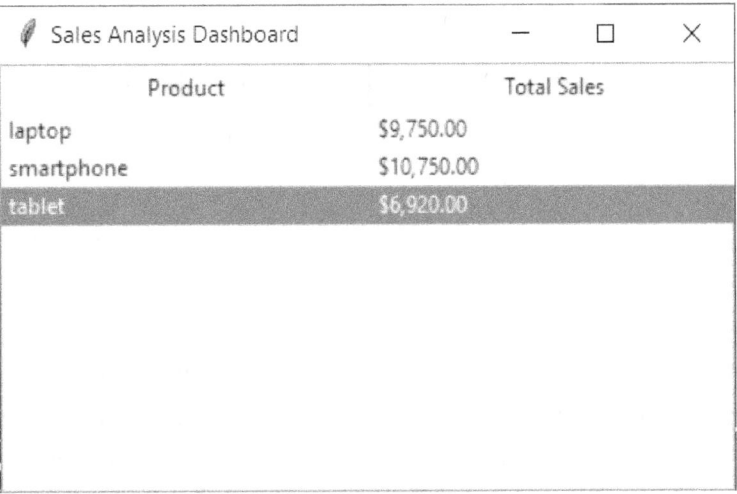

Explanation of the Code
- Class Definition (SalesApp): The class encapsulates all functionality related to the GUI. It initializes the main window, sets up widgets, and populates them with data.
- Window Setup: The __init__ method sets the title and size of the main window and calls setup_widgets to initialize the GUI components.
- Widgets Setup (setup_widgets): This method creates a Treeview widget from the ttk module, which is used to display the sales data in a table-like format. Headers for product, total sales, and average price are set up.
- Data Population (populate_data): This method calculates total sales, total units, and average price using dictionary comprehensions and loops over the sales data. The results are then inserted into the Treeview for display.
- Running the Application: At the bottom, a Tkinter root window is created, an instance of SalesApp is initialized with this root, and the main loop is started to run the application.

GUI Features and User Interaction
- Data Display: The sales data is displayed in a structured Treeview, making it easy for users to view the aggregated results.
- Scalability: New data entries or analysis metrics can be added to the populate_data method, and the GUI will update accordingly.

- Styling and Layout: The application uses the default styling of Tkinter and ttk, which can be further customized for a more appealing look.

This GUI application serves as a basic dashboard for viewing sales analysis results, demonstrating how to integrate Python data manipulation with Tkinter for interactive applications.

Example 2.3
Combining Customer Data

Merging dictionaries is a common task in Python, particularly useful when dealing with data that comes from multiple sources and needs to be combined into a single structure for processing or analysis. Starting with Python 3.9, you can merge dictionaries using the new merge (|) and update (|=) operators. Before Python 3.9, merging dictionaries could be achieved using the update() method or by unpacking dictionaries in a single expression with **.

Suppose you are working with customer data in a marketing department. You have customer profiles stored in one dictionary and additional customer preferences in another. Your task is to merge these dictionaries to create a unified view of each customer's data.

Setup the Basic Data Structures

Here's how you might set up and merge customer data using both Python 3.9+ syntax with the merge operator and the traditional method:

```
# Data from the customer registration form
customer_profiles = {
    "001": {"name": "Alice Johnson", "email": "alice.johnson@example.com"},
    "002": {"name": "Bob Smith", "email": "bob.smith@example.com"}
}

# Data from a customer survey on preferences
customer_preferences = {
    "001": {"newsletter": "weekly", "interests": ["technology", "finance"]},
    "002": {"newsletter": "monthly", "interests": ["sports", "travel"]}
}

# Merging dictionaries in Python 3.9+ using the merge operator
```

```
combined_customers = {cid: customer_profiles[cid] | customer_preferences[cid] 
for cid in customer_profiles}

# For those using versions prior to Python 3.9, merging with the unpacking 
method:
combined_customers_legacy = {
    cid: {**customer_profiles[cid], **customer_preferences[cid]} for cid in 
customer_profiles
}

# Display the merged data
for customer_id, data in combined_customers.items():
    print(f"Customer ID: {customer_id}")
    for key, value in data.items():
        print(f"  {key}: {value}")
    print()

# Output:
# Customer ID: 001
#   name: Alice Johnson
#   email: alice.johnson@example.com
#   newsletter: weekly
#   interests: ['technology', 'finance']
#
# Customer ID: 002
#   name: Bob Smith
#   email: bob.smith@example.com
#   newsletter: monthly
#   interests: ['sports', 'travel']
```

Explanation

- Data Sources: We start with two dictionaries: customer_profiles, which contains basic customer data, and customer_preferences, which includes data from a survey about their preferences.
- Merging Dictionaries:
    - Python 3.9+: The example uses the new | operator to merge dictionaries. This operator makes it straightforward to merge two dictionaries into a new one.
    - Pre-Python 3.9: The example shows how to use the unpacking method (**) to achieve the same result for those on older Python versions.
- Iterating for Output: The script iterates through the combined dictionary to print each customer's complete profile.

Benefits of Merging Dictionaries
- Efficiency: Merging dictionaries is typically more efficient and readable than manually iterating through keys and setting values.
- Clarity: Using the merge operator or the unpacking method provides clear, concise syntax that is easy to understand.
- Flexibility: Merging allows you to easily combine data from multiple sources, enhancing data manipulation capabilities in Python.

Conclusion
This example demonstrates how merging dictionaries can be used to effectively combine data from multiple sources, providing a powerful tool for data aggregation tasks commonly required in real-world applications like data analysis, customer relationship management, and more. Whether you're working in a business environment or managing complex data for scientific research, understanding how to merge dictionaries efficiently is an essential skill in Python programming.

Example 2.4
GUI Tkinter for Combining Customer Data
To create a graphical user interface (GUI) using Tkinter that integrates and displays customer profile and preference data, we will develop a Python class-based application. This GUI will facilitate the viewing of merged customer information, enhancing user interaction for customer service or marketing purposes.

Step 1: Define the GUI Class for Customer Data Integration
We'll set up the main class for our GUI, which will handle initializing the main window and provide methods for displaying the merged customer data.

```
import tkinter as tk
from tkinter import ttk

class CustomerProfileApp:
    def __init__(self, master):
        self.master = master
        self.master.title("Customer Profile Manager")
        self.master.geometry("600x400")
```

```python
        # Initialize customer data
        self.customer_profiles = {
            "001": {"name": "Alice Johnson", "email": "alice.johnson@example.com"},
            "002": {"name": "Bob Smith", "email": "bob.smith@example.com"}
        }

        self.customer_preferences = {
            "001": {"newsletter": "weekly", "interests": ["technology", "finance"]},
            "002": {"newsletter": "monthly", "interests": ["sports", "travel"]}
        }

        # Merge customer data
        self.combined_customers = {
            cid: {**self.customer_profiles[cid], **self.customer_preferences[cid]} for cid in self.customer_profiles
        }

        # GUI Setup
        self.setup_widgets()

    def setup_widgets(self):
        # Treeview for displaying customer data
        self.tree = ttk.Treeview(self.master, columns=('Customer ID', 'Name', 'Email', 'Newsletter', 'Interests'), show='headings')
        self.tree.heading('Customer ID', text='Customer ID')
        self.tree.heading('Name', text='Name')
        self.tree.heading('Email', text='Email')
        self.tree.heading('Newsletter', text='Newsletter')
        self.tree.heading('Interests', text='Interests')
        self.tree.pack(fill=tk.BOTH, expand=True, padx=20, pady=20)

        # Button to refresh data
        ttk.Button(self.master, text="Refresh Data", command=self.populate_treeview).pack(pady=10)

        # Initially populate the Treeview
        self.populate_treeview()

    def populate_treeview(self):
        self.tree.delete(*self.tree.get_children())  # Clear existing data
        for cid, data in self.combined_customers.items():
            interests = ', '.join(data['interests'])
            self.tree.insert('', tk.END, values=(cid, data['name'], data['email'], data['newsletter'], interests))

if __name__ == "__main__":
    root = tk.Tk()
    app = CustomerProfileApp(root)
    root.mainloop()
```

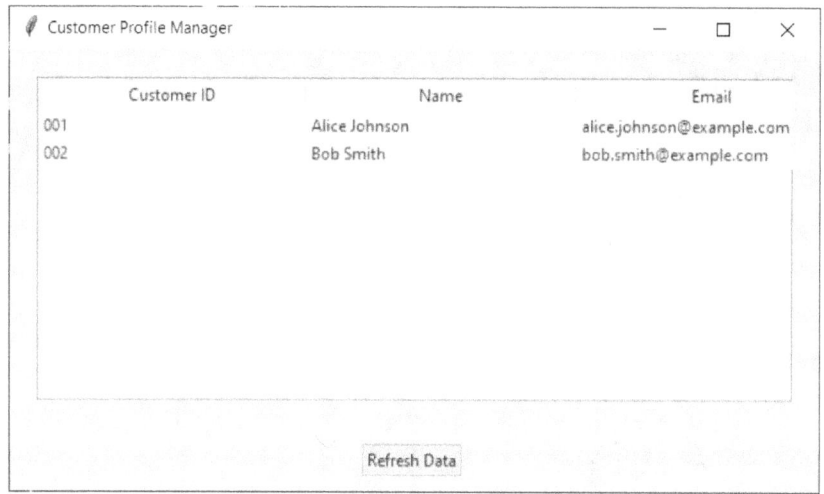

Explanation of the Code
1. Class Definition (CustomerProfileApp):
   Initializes the main window (master) and sets up GUI components for interacting with the combined customer data.
2. Widget Setup (setup_widgets):
   Configures the GUI layout, adding a Treeview to display the customer data and a button to refresh the data in the view. This setup allows for a structured display of customer information including their preferences.
3. Displaying Customer Data (populate_treeview):
   Refreshes the Treeview with the latest data by iterating over the combined_customers dictionary. It formats customer interests from a list to a string for display.

Features of the GUI
- Interactive Data Display: The GUI provides a user-friendly way to view detailed customer profiles and preferences.
- Dynamic Updates: Users can interact with the data through the GUI, such as refreshing the data displayed.
- Efficient Data Handling: The application efficiently manages and displays complex data structures, which enhances data accessibility and management.

This GUI application effectively demonstrates how to integrate and visualize customer data in a practical and user-friendly interface, making it an excellent tool for customer relationship management or marketing analysis.

Example 2.5
Managing Configuration Settings
In Python, copying dictionaries is a common operation, especially when you want to modify a copy of a dictionary without altering the original. This is useful in scenarios where you need to keep the original data intact for reference or further use while working on a mutable copy of the data. Let's explore a real-world example involving configuration settings for an application where copying a dictionary is crucial.

Imagine you are developing a software application that allows users to have both a default configuration and a user-specific configuration that overrides the default settings. You would typically start with a default configuration dictionary, and then create a copy of this dictionary for each user, which can be modified based on user preferences.

Setup the Basic Configuration
Here's how you might manage configuration settings using dictionary copying:

```
import copy

# Default configuration for an application
default_config = {
    "theme": "light",
    "notifications": True,
    "language": "English",
    "privacy": {
        "location": False,
        "search_history": True
    }
}

# Function to create a user-specific configuration
def create_user_config(user_preferences):
    # Create a deep copy of the default configuration
    user_config = copy.deepcopy(default_config)

    # Apply user-specific preferences
    user_config.update(user_preferences)

    return user_config

# Example user preferences that override some of the default settings
alice_preferences = {
    "theme": "dark",
```

```
    "privacy": {
        "location": True
    }
}

# Create a user-specific configuration for Alice
alice_config = create_user_config(alice_preferences)

# Display configurations
print("Default Configuration:")
print(default_config)

print("\nAlice's Configuration:")
print(alice_config)

# Output:
# Default Configuration:
# {'theme': 'light', 'notifications': True, 'language': 'English', 'privacy':
{'location': False, 'search_history': True}}
#
# Alice's Configuration:
# {'theme': 'dark', 'notifications': True, 'language': 'English', 'privacy':
{'location': True}}
```

Explanation

- Deep Copy: It's crucial to use copy.deepcopy() when the dictionary contains nested dictionaries, as in the privacy settings. A shallow copy (dict.copy()) would not suffice because it would result in the nested dictionaries still being shared between the original and the copy, which can lead to unintended side effects.
- Updating Configuration: Once a deep copy of the default configuration is made for a user, it is then updated with the user's preferences, which might only partially override the default settings.
- Separation of Data: This approach ensures that the user-specific configurations are independent of each other and the default configuration, thus any changes made to one user's configuration do not affect another.

Benefits of Copying Dictionaries

- Data Integrity: Copying dictionaries ensures that the original data remains unchanged, which is crucial when the original serves as a template or base configuration.

- Flexibility: Users can safely modify their configurations without the risk of affecting the system-wide defaults or other users' settings.

Conclusion

This example illustrates the practical application of copying dictionaries in Python, particularly with copy.deepcopy(), in settings management for applications. Such functionality is invaluable in many areas of software development, including user interfaces, application settings management, and any scenario where customizable user data needs to be derived from a standard template. Understanding how to copy dictionaries properly is essential for ensuring robust and error-free code.

Example 2.6
Tkinter for Managing Configuration Settings

To develop a rich graphical user interface (GUI) using Tkinter that allows real-time interaction with user-specific application settings, we will create a Python class-based application. This GUI will enable users to view and modify their preferences dynamically, reflecting updates immediately.

Step 1: Define the GUI Class for Configuration Management

The main class will manage the initialization of the GUI window and provide methods for interacting with and displaying user configurations.

```
import tkinter as tk
from tkinter import ttk, messagebox, simpledialog, BooleanVar
import copy

class ConfigManagerApp:
    def __init__(self, master):
        self.master = master
        self.master.title("Configuration Manager")
        self.master.geometry("500x400")

        # Default and user configuration setup
        self.default_config = {
            "theme": "light",
            "notifications": True,
            "language": "English",
            "privacy": {
                "location": False,
                "search_history": True
```

```python
            }
        }

        # Placeholder for user configuration
        self.user_config = copy.deepcopy(self.default_config)

        # GUI Layout
        self.setup_widgets()

    def setup_widgets(self):
        ttk.Label(self.master, text="User Configuration", font=('Arial', 16)).pack(pady=20)

        # Theme Configuration
        ttk.Label(self.master, text="Theme:").pack()
        self.theme_var = tk.StringVar(value=self.user_config['theme'])
        ttk.Radiobutton(self.master, text='Light', variable=self.theme_var, value='light', command=self.update_config).pack()
        ttk.Radiobutton(self.master, text='Dark', variable=self.theme_var, value='dark', command=self.update_config).pack()

        # Notification Configuration
        ttk.Label(self.master, text="Notifications:").pack()
        self.notif_var = BooleanVar(value=self.user_config['notifications'])
        ttk.Checkbutton(self.master, text="Enable Notifications", variable=self.notif_var, command=self.update_config).pack()

        # Privacy Settings
        ttk.Label(self.master, text="Location Access:").pack()
        self.location_var = BooleanVar(value=self.user_config['privacy']['location'])
        ttk.Checkbutton(self.master, text="Allow Location", variable=self.location_var, command=self.update_config).pack()

        # Button to reset to default
        ttk.Button(self.master, text="Reset to Default", command=self.reset_to_default).pack(pady=20)

    def update_config(self):
        # Update user configuration based on GUI inputs
        self.user_config['theme'] = self.theme_var.get()
        self.user_config['notifications'] = self.notif_var.get()
        self.user_config['privacy']['location'] = self.location_var.get()

    def reset_to_default(self):
        # Reset user configuration to default settings
        self.user_config = copy.deepcopy(self.default_config)
        self.refresh_gui()

    def refresh_gui(self):
        # Refresh GUI elements to match current config
```

```
            self.theme_var.set(self.user_config['theme'])
            self.notif_var.set(self.user_config['notifications'])
            self.location_var.set(self.user_config['privacy']['location'])

if __name__ == "__main__":
    root = tk.Tk()
    app = ConfigManagerApp(root)
    root.mainloop()
```

Explanation of the Code

1. Class Definition (ConfigManagerApp):
   Initializes the main window and sets up GUI components for interacting with configuration settings.
2. Widget Setup (setup_widgets):
   Configures the GUI layout, adding controls (radio buttons, checkboxes) for each configuration setting, such as theme and notifications, and a button to reset settings to default.
3. Updating and Resetting Configurations:
   - update_config modifies the user configuration based on the user's selections.
   - reset_to_default restores the configuration to the initial default settings and updates the GUI to reflect these changes.
4. Dynamic Feedback and GUI Refresh:
   - When settings are changed, the GUI controls are updated to reflect the current settings, providing immediate visual feedback.
   - This dynamic interaction ensures that users can see and modify their settings in real-time, enhancing usability.

Features of the GUI

- Interactive Configuration: The GUI allows users to interactively change their configuration settings with immediate updates.
- Real-Time Updates: Changes to settings are immediately reflected in the GUI, ensuring that the user always sees the most current configuration.
- Ease of Use: The GUI is designed to be intuitive, with clear labels and easy-to-use controls, making configuration management accessible to all users.

This GUI application provides a practical and user-friendly interface for managing application settings, demonstrating how GUIs can enhance user interaction with software settings, making them more engaging and easier to manage.

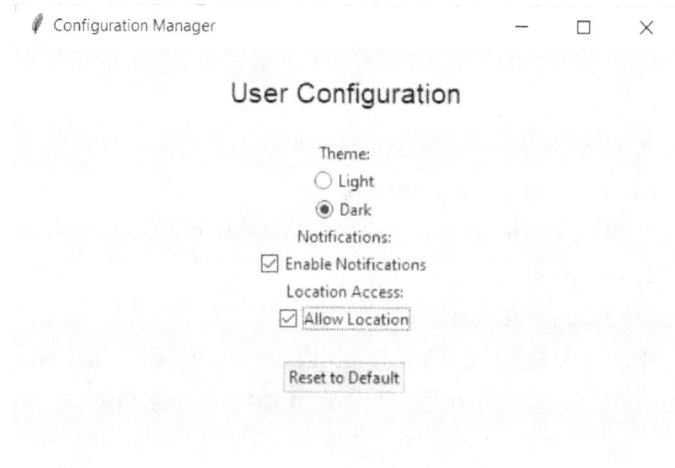

Example 2.7
Session Management in a Web Application
In Python, clearing a dictionary is an operation that removes all items from the dictionary, making it empty. This can be useful in scenarios where you need to reuse or reset a dictionary within the same context or scope without creating a new dictionary object. Here's a practical example involving session management for a web application, where clearing a dictionary helps manage user sessions efficiently.

Suppose you are developing a web application where user sessions need to be managed manually. Each session might include various attributes like user credentials, time stamps, permissions, and other user-specific data. In cases where a user logs out or when a session expires, you may want to clear the session data without deleting the session object itself.

Setup the Session Structure
Here's how you might implement session management that includes clearing sessions:

```
# Simulated session dictionary for multiple users
sessions = {
    'user1': {'username': 'alice', 'access_level': 'admin', 'last_login': '2024-05-03'},
    'user2': {'username': 'bob', 'access_level': 'user', 'last_login': '2024-05-02'}
```

```
}

# Function to simulate user login which creates session data
def login(user_id, username, access_level):
    sessions[user_id] = {'username': username, 'access_level': access_level,
'last_login': '2024-05-04'}
    print(f"User {username} logged in with access level {access_level}.")

# Function to simulate user logout which clears session data
def logout(user_id):
    # Clear the specific user's session data
    sessions[user_id].clear()
    print(f"Session for user_id {user_id} cleared.")

# Function to display all session data
def display_sessions():
    print("Current Sessions:")
    for user_id, session_data in sessions.items():
        if session_data:
            print(f"{user_id}: {session_data}")
        else:
            print(f"{user_id}: No active session")

# Example usage
login('user1', 'alice', 'admin')
display_sessions()
logout('user1')
display_sessions()

# Output:
# User alice logged in with access level admin.
# Current Sessions:
# user1: {'username': 'alice', 'access_level': 'admin', 'last_login': '2024-05-04'}
# user2: {'username': 'bob', 'access_level': 'user', 'last_login': '2024-05-02'}
# Session for user_id user1 cleared.
# Current Sessions:
# user1: No active session
# user2: {'username': 'bob', 'access_level': 'user', 'last_login': '2024-05-02'}
```

Explanation
- Session Dictionary: The sessions dictionary maps user IDs to their respective session data. Each session data itself is a dictionary containing user-specific information.
- Login Function: Adds or updates session data for a given user.
- Logout Function: Clears the session data for a specified user using the .clear() method. This method empties the dictionary but does not delete the dictionary object itself, allowing the session ID to remain valid and reusable.

- Display Function: Shows all current session data, checking if any user data exists or if the session is empty.

Benefits of Clearing Dictionaries
- Resource Management: Clearing dictionaries can help manage resources effectively, especially in environments like web servers where memory and data management are crucial.
- Data Security: In web applications, clearing session data ensures that sensitive information is not left accessible after a user logs out, enhancing security.

Conclusion
This example illustrates the practical use of clearing dictionaries in session management for web applications. By using the .clear() method, the application can efficiently handle login and logout operations, ensuring that user data is managed securely and resources are not wasted. This approach is particularly useful in maintaining the integrity of session IDs while ensuring that all associated data is reset appropriately.

Example 2.8
GUI Tkinter Session Management in a Web Application
To create a rich graphical user interface (GUI) in Tkinter that simulates user session management with login and logout functionality, we can develop a Python class-based application. This GUI will enable users to interactively log in, view active sessions, and log out, updating session data in real time.

Step 1: Define the GUI Class for Session Management
We'll start by setting up the main class for our GUI, which will manage initializing the main window and providing methods for user login, logout, and displaying session data.

```
import tkinter as tk
from tkinter import ttk, simpledialog, messagebox

class SessionManagerApp:
    def __init__(self, master):
        self.master = master
        self.master.title("Session Manager")
        self.master.geometry("400x300")
```

```python
        self.sessions = {
            'user1': {'username': 'alice', 'access_level': 'admin', 'last_login': '2024-05-03'},
            'user2': {'username': 'bob', 'access_level': 'user', 'last_login': '2024-05-02'}
        }

        self.setup_widgets()

    def setup_widgets(self):
        ttk.Button(self.master, text="Login User", command=self.login_user).pack(pady=10)
        ttk.Button(self.master, text="Logout User", command=self.logout_user).pack(pady=10)
        ttk.Button(self.master, text="Display Sessions", command=self.display_sessions).pack(pady=10)

        self.text_display = tk.Text(self.master, height=10, width=50)
        self.text_display.pack(pady=20)

    def login_user(self):
        user_id = simpledialog.askstring("Login", "Enter user ID:")
        username = simpledialog.askstring("Login", "Enter username:")
        access_level = simpledialog.askstring("Login", "Enter access level:")
        self.login(user_id, username, access_level)
        self.display_sessions()

    def logout_user(self):
        user_id = simpledialog.askstring("Logout", "Enter user ID to logout:")
        self.logout(user_id)
        self.display_sessions()

    def display_sessions(self):
        self.text_display.delete('1.0', tk.END)
        self.text_display.insert(tk.END, "Current Sessions:\n")
        for user_id, session_data in self.sessions.items():
            if session_data:
                self.text_display.insert(tk.END, f"{user_id}: {session_data}\n")
            else:
                self.text_display.insert(tk.END, f"{user_id}: No active session\n")

    def login(self, user_id, username, access_level):
        if user_id and username and access_level:
            self.sessions[user_id] = {'username': username, 'access_level': access_level, 'last_login': '2024-05-04'}
            messagebox.showinfo("Login", f"User {username} logged in with access level {access_level}.")

    def logout(self, user_id):
        if user_id in self.sessions:
```

```
            self.sessions[user_id].clear()
            messagebox.showinfo("Logout", f"Session for user_id {user_id} cleared.")
if __name__ == "__main__":
    root = tk.Tk()
    app = SessionManagerApp(root)
    root.mainloop()
```

Explanation of the Code

1. Class Definition (SessionManagerApp):
   Initializes the main window and sets up GUI components to interact with session data. Includes buttons for login, logout, and displaying sessions and a text display area for session information.
2. Widget Setup (setup_widgets):
   Configures the GUI layout with buttons and a text display area. Each button is linked to a specific functionality: logging in a user, logging out a user, and displaying all session data.
3. Interactive Session Management:
   - login_user and logout_user trigger dialog prompts for user input and then call login and logout functions respectively, reflecting changes immediately in the GUI.
   - display_sessions updates the text display area to show current session statuses, allowing real-time monitoring of active sessions.

Features of the GUI

- Real-Time Interaction: The GUI allows for dynamic interaction with session data, including logging in and logging out users.
- Immediate Feedback: Users receive instant feedback through the text display area and message boxes, enhancing usability.
- Clear and User-Friendly Interface: The straightforward layout makes it easy for users to manage sessions effectively.

This GUI application provides a practical demonstration of how a graphical interface can enhance interaction with session data, making session management more accessible and user-friendly.

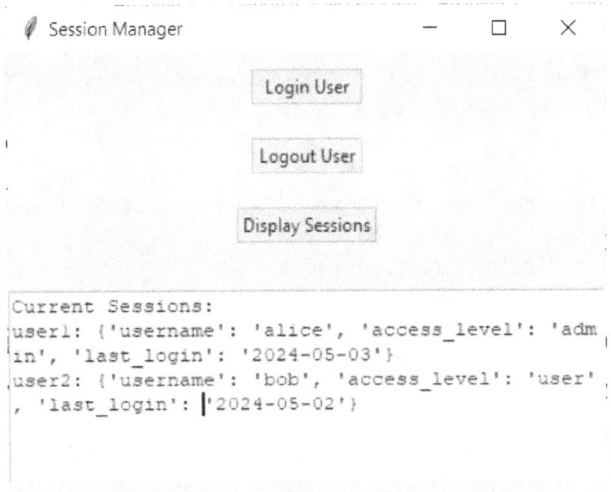

Example 2.9
E-commerce Application Customer Preferences
In Python, the get() method on dictionaries is an essential tool for safely accessing dictionary values. It provides a way to specify a default value that is returned if the specified key is not found in the dictionary. This prevents the program from raising a KeyError, which would occur if you tried to access a key that does not exist using the standard bracket notation.

Let's explore a practical real-world example using the get() method in the context of processing customer data in an e-commerce application. This example involves checking for customer preferences on receiving promotional emails and handling missing data gracefully.

Suppose you are developing an e-commerce application where you need to handle various customer preferences for marketing, such as whether they want to receive promotional emails. The customer data, including preferences, is stored in a dictionary. Not all customers might have set this preference, so using get() allows the application to handle missing preferences gracefully by providing a default value.

Setup Customer Data and Preference Check
Here's how you might implement this using the get() method:

```
# Customer data stored in a dictionary
customers = {
```

```
    "001": {"name": "Alice Johnson", "email": "alice@example.com", "promo_opt_in": True},
    "002": {"name": "Bob Smith", "email": "bob@example.com"},  # No 'promo_opt_in' key
    "003": {"name": "Carol White", "email": "carol@example.com", "promo_opt_in": False}
}

# Function to check if a customer wants to receive promotional emails
def check_promo_preference(customer_id):
    # Get the customer dictionary using the customer ID
    customer = customers.get(customer_id, None)
    if customer is None:
        print(f"No customer found with ID {customer_id}.")
        return
    
    # Use get() to safely access 'promo_opt_in' and assume False if not found
    promo_opt_in = customer.get('promo_opt_in', False)
    
    if promo_opt_in:
        print(f"Customer {customer['name']} has opted in to receive promotional emails.")
    else:
        print(f"Customer {customer['name']} has opted out or not set promotional preferences.")

# Example Usage
check_promo_preference("001")
check_promo_preference("002")
check_promo_preference("003")
check_promo_preference("004")  # Non-existent customer ID

# Output:
# Customer Alice Johnson has opted in to receive promotional emails.
# Customer Bob Smith has opted out or not set promotional preferences.
# Customer Carol White has opted out or not set promotional preferences.
# No customer found with ID 004.
```

Explanation
- Customer Data: The customers dictionary maps customer IDs to another dictionary that includes their name, email, and an optional promo_opt_in key indicating their preference for receiving promotional content.
- get() for Default Values: When accessing the promo_opt_in key, the get() method is used with a default value of False. This means if the promo_opt_in key is missing, the function assumes the customer has not opted in.
- Handling Non-existent Keys: Another get() is used to retrieve the customer dictionary from the main customers dictionary. Here, get() returns None if the customer ID does not exist, allowing the function to handle this gracefully.

Benefits of the get() Method
- Safety and Robustness: Prevents crashes due to missing keys by providing a mechanism to return a default value.
- Simplicity: Reduces the need for explicit key existence checks (like using in or not in) and makes the code cleaner and easier to understand.

Conclusion
This example shows how the get() method can be effectively used in handling potentially incomplete data in application development, particularly in situations where user preferences might not always be set. Using get() helps in writing more robust and fault-tolerant code, crucial for applications that involve user input or external data sources.

Example 2.10
GUI Tkinter E-commerce Application Customer Preferences
To create a rich, real-time graphical user interface (GUI) using Tkinter that enables users to interact with customer data and check promotional preferences, we'll build a Python class-based application. This GUI will allow users to input a customer ID, check the customer's preference for receiving promotional emails, and display the result directly in the interface.

Step 1: Define the GUI Class for Customer Data Interaction
We will define a main class for our GUI, which will manage initializing the main window and provide methods for user interaction with the customer data.

```python
import tkinter as tk
from tkinter import ttk, messagebox, simpledialog

class CustomerPreferenceApp:
    def __init__(self, master):
        self.master = master
        self.master.title("Customer Preference Manager")
        self.master.geometry("400x300")

        # Initialize customer data
        self.customers = {
            "001": {"name": "Alice Johnson", "email": "alice@example.com", "promo_opt_in": True},
            "002": {"name": "Bob Smith", "email": "bob@example.com"},  # No 'promo_opt_in' key
```

```python
            "003": {"name": "Carol White", "email": "carol@example.com", "promo_opt_in": False}
        }

        # GUI Setup
        self.setup_widgets()

    def setup_widgets(self):
        # Label for instruction
        ttk.Label(self.master, text="Enter Customer ID to check promo preferences:", font=('Arial', 12)).pack(pady=20)

        # Entry field for customer ID
        self.customer_id_entry = ttk.Entry(self.master, width=20, font=('Arial', 12))
        self.customer_id_entry.pack(pady=10)

        # Button to check preference
        ttk.Button(self.master, text="Check Preference", command=self.check_preference).pack(pady=10)

        # Label to display results
        self.result_label = ttk.Label(self.master, text="", font=('Arial', 12))
        self.result_label.pack(pady=20)

    def check_preference(self):
        customer_id = self.customer_id_entry.get()
        result = self.check_promo_preference(customer_id)
        self.result_label.config(text=result)

    def check_promo_preference(self, customer_id):
        customer = self.customers.get(customer_id, None)
        if customer is None:
            return f"No customer found with ID {customer_id}."

        promo_opt_in = customer.get('promo_opt_in', False)
        if promo_opt_in:
            return f"Customer {customer['name']} has opted in to receive promotional emails."
        else:
            return f"Customer {customer['name']} has opted out or not set promotional preferences."

if __name__ == "__main__":
    root = tk.Tk()
    app = CustomerPreferenceApp(root)
    root.mainloop()
```

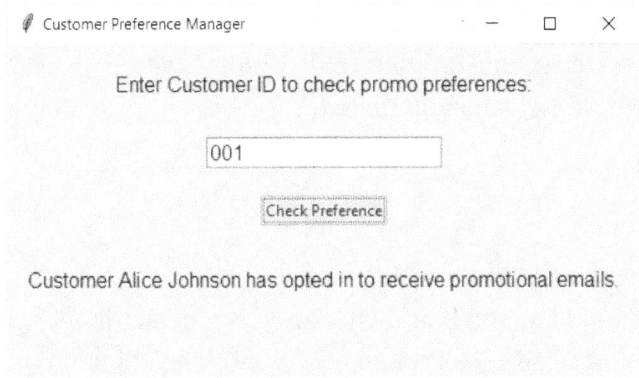

Explanation of the Code

1. Class Definition (CustomerPreferenceApp):
   Initializes the main window (master) and sets up GUI components to interact with customer promotional preferences.
2. Widget Setup (setup_widgets):
   Configures the GUI layout with an entry field for inputting a customer ID, a button to initiate the preference check, and a label to display results. This allows users to dynamically interact with the data.
3. Interaction Methods:
   - check_preference retrieves the customer ID from the entry field, calls check_promo_preference to get the result, and updates the result label accordingly.
   - Checking Promotional Preferences:
   - check_promo_preference checks the dictionary for the customer ID, safely retrieves the promo opt-in preference using the get method, and formats a response based on whether the customer has opted in or out.

Features of the GUI

- User Input and Dynamic Feedback: Users can enter a customer ID and immediately see whether that customer has opted in to receive promotional emails.
- Immediate Error Handling: Provides feedback if a customer ID is not found, enhancing usability and error management.
- Clear and User-Friendly Interface: The straightforward design makes it easy for users to interact with the application and understand the displayed information.

This GUI application provides an intuitive way for staff or marketers to quickly check customer preferences regarding promotional communications, making management of marketing efforts more efficient and targeted.

Example 2.11
Counting Item Occurrences in Store Inventory
In Python, the setdefault() method on dictionaries is a versatile tool that not only fetches the value of a key but also sets the dictionary key with a default value if the key does not exist. This method is particularly useful when you need to ensure that a key exists in the dictionary without having to explicitly check for its presence first.

Let's explore a real-world example using the setdefault() method in the context of counting occurrences of items in a dataset. This example involves creating a frequency dictionary for various items in a store's inventory, which is a common task in data analysis for understanding inventory distribution, customer preferences, or even for general data categorization.

Imagine you're managing a store and you receive shipments that contain various items. You want to keep track of how many of each item you receive to manage your inventory better.

Setup and Use of setdefault()
Here's how you might implement this counting using the setdefault() method:

```python
# List of items received in various shipments
shipments = ['apple', 'banana', 'apple', 'orange', 'banana', 'apple']

# Dictionary to store the count of each item
item_count = {}

# Count each item using setdefault
for item in shipments:
    item_count.setdefault(item, 0)
    item_count[item] += 1

# Display the item counts
print("Item Counts:")
for item, count in item_count.items():
    print(f"{item}: {count}")
```

```
# Output:
# Item Counts:
# apple: 3
# banana: 2
# orange: 1
```

Explanation
- Inventory Data: The shipments list represents items received in various shipments.
- Using setdefault(): For each item in the list, setdefault() is used to initialize the count of that item to 0 if it hasn't been added to item_count yet. After initializing (if necessary), it increments the count of the item.

This approach is particularly elegant because setdefault() handles both checking for the existence of the key and initializing it in a single operation, which simplifies the code and makes it more efficient than checking if the key exists and then adding it if it does not.

Benefits of the setdefault() Method
- Efficiency: Combines the functionality of checking for a key and initializing it if absent, which can make code more concise and potentially faster.
- Convenience: Reduces the number of lines needed to perform common tasks like building histograms or counting occurrences.

Conclusion

This example illustrates the practical utility of the setdefault() method for managing and analyzing data, such as counting occurrences of items in a dataset. By simplifying the process of updating dictionary entries, setdefault() allows developers to write cleaner and more efficient Python code, especially useful in data processing and inventory management applications. The method is ideally suited for situations where you need to ensure that a dictionary key is initialized the first time it is encountered in a processing loop.

Example 2.12
GUI Tkinter Counting Item Occurrences in Store Inventory
To create a graphical user interface (GUI) in Tkinter that allows real-time interaction with inventory data derived from shipment items and demonstrates counting each item's occurrences, we will develop a Python class-based application. This GUI will enable users to add items to shipments dynamically and view updated counts instantly.

Step 1: Define the GUI Class for Inventory Management
We'll start by setting up the main class for our GUI, which will manage the initialization of the main window and provide methods for user interaction with the shipment data.

```python
import tkinter as tk
from tkinter import ttk, simpledialog, messagebox

class ShipmentCounterApp:
    def __init__(self, master):
        self.master = master
        self.master.title("Shipment Counter Manager")
        self.master.geometry("400x300")

        # Initialize the shipment list and item count dictionary
        self.shipments = ['apple', 'banana', 'apple', 'orange', 'banana', 'apple']
        self.item_count = {}

        # Count items in the initial list
        self.count_items()

        # GUI Setup
        self.setup_widgets()

    def setup_widgets(self):
        # Label for instruction
        ttk.Label(self.master, text="Current Item Counts:", font=('Arial', 14)).pack(pady=10)

        # Text box to display counts
        self.text_display = tk.Text(self.master, height=10, width=30)
        self.text_display.pack(pady=10)

        # Button to add a new item
        ttk.Button(self.master, text="Add New Item", command=self.add_item).pack(pady=10)

        # Initially display the current counts
        self.display_counts()
```

```
    def count_items(self):
        """ Count each item using setdefault """
        for item in self.shipments:
            self.item_count.setdefault(item, 0)
            self.item_count[item] += 1

    def display_counts(self):
        """ Display the current item counts in the text widget """
        self.text_display.delete('1.0', tk.END)
        for item, count in self.item_count.items():
            self.text_display.insert(tk.END, f"{item}: {count}\n")

    def add_item(self):
        """ Prompt user to add a new item to the shipments and update counts """
        new_item = simpledialog.askstring("Add Item", "Enter the item name:")
        if new_item:
            self.shipments.append(new_item)
            self.item_count.setdefault(new_item, 0)
            self.item_count[new_item] += 1
            self.display_counts()
        else:
            messagebox.showwarning("Warning", "No item entered!")

if __name__ == "__main__":
    root = tk.Tk()
    app = ShipmentCounterApp(root)
    root.mainloop()
```

Explanation of the Code

1. Class Definition (ShipmentCounterApp):
   Initializes the main window and sets up GUI components to interact with shipment data, allowing for the addition of new items and viewing updated counts.
2. Widget Setup (setup_widgets):
   Configures the GUI layout, adding a text display for item counts and a button for adding new items. Provides a clear and interactive way for users to manage inventory.
3. Item Counting and Display (count_items and display_counts):
   - count_items processes the current list of shipments to update the count of each item.
   - display_counts updates the text display widget with the latest counts, allowing users to see real-time data as items are added.
4. Adding New Items (add_item):

Prompts the user to enter a new item name and adds it to the shipments list. Updates the item counts and refreshes the display. If no item is entered, it shows a warning.

Features of the GUI
- Dynamic Interaction: Users can dynamically add new items to the shipment list and see the updated counts instantly, enhancing real-time data interaction.
- Clear and User-Friendly Interface: The GUI is designed to be intuitive, with simple instructions and immediate feedback on actions taken.
- Robust Data Management: The application effectively manages and displays shipment data, making it a practical tool for inventory or shipment management scenarios.

This GUI application provides a practical demonstration of how a graphical interface can enhance interaction with data, particularly in inventory management, by making it more engaging and accessible.

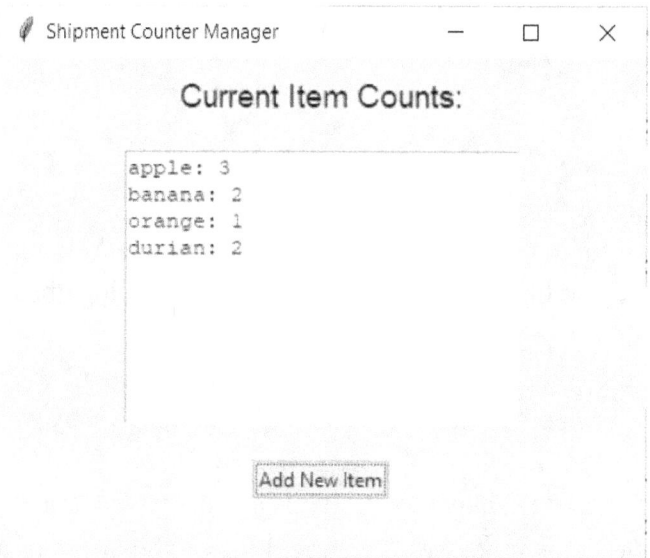

ADDITIONAL OPERATIONS AND FEATURES

Dictionary Views:
Dictionary views provide dynamic views on the dictionary's keys, values, or key-value pairs, which reflect changes made to the dictionary.
- keys(): Returns a view of all the keys in the dictionary.
- values(): Returns a view of all the values in the dictionary.
- items(): Returns a view of all the key-value pairs in the dictionary.

```
keys_view = my_dict.keys()
values_view = my_dict.values()
items_view = my_dict.items()
```

These views can be useful when you want to perform operations on keys, values, or items without creating a separate list.

Dictionary Membership Testing:
You can use the in and not in operators to test for membership in keys.

```
if "name" in my_dict:
    print("Name is present in the dictionary")
```

Nested Dictionaries:
Dictionaries can contain other dictionaries as values.

```
nested_dict = {"info": {"name": "Alice", "age": 25}, "address": {"city": "New York", "zip": "10001"}}
```

Dictionary Methods:
Python dictionaries come with various methods to manipulate and access data efficiently. Some important methods include:
- update(): Updates the dictionary with the elements from another dictionary or from an iterable of key-value pairs.
- fromkeys(): Creates a new dictionary with keys from an iterable and values set to a default value.
- copy(): Returns a shallow copy of the dictionary.
- clear(): Removes all items from the dictionary.

Dictionary Sorting:
While dictionaries themselves are unordered collections, you can sort them by their keys or values.

```
sorted_dict = sorted(my_dict.items())   # Sorts dictionary by keys
sorted_dict_by_values = sorted(my_dict.items(), key=lambda x: x[1])   # Sorts dictionary by values
```

Hashability:
Since dictionary keys must be immutable, they are usually hashable. This means they can be used as keys in another dictionary or as elements in a set.

Dictionary Aliasing:
Be cautious when assigning one dictionary to another variable. Changes to one dictionary may affect the other.

```
dict1 = {"a": 1, "b": 2}
dict2 = dict1
dict2["c"] = 3
print(dict1)   # Output: {'a': 1, 'b': 2, 'c': 3}
```

Python dictionaries are incredibly flexible and powerful data structures that can be used in a wide range of applications, from simple key-value mappings to complex data modeling and manipulation tasks. Understanding their various operations and features is essential for effective Python programming.

Example 2.13
Real-Time Inventory Tracking System
In Python, dictionaries provide dynamic views on the keys, values, and key-value pairs through the .keys(), .values(), and .items() methods, respectively. These views are dynamic in that they reflect changes to the dictionary in real-time, making them very useful in scenarios where you need to monitor dictionary modifications during runtime.

Let's explore a real-world example where dynamic views of a dictionary are used in a simple inventory tracking system for a small business. This system monitors changes in inventory levels and updates them in real-time as sales are made or new stock is added.

Setup the Inventory and Operations

Here's how you might implement this system:

```python
# Initial inventory of products
inventory = {
    "laptops": 30,
    "smartphones": 50,
    "tablets": 20
}

# Displaying initial inventory
print("Initial Inventory:")
for product, quantity in inventory.items():
    print(f"{product}: {quantity}")

# Create dynamic views
inventory_keys = inventory.keys()
inventory_values = inventory.values()
inventory_items = inventory.items()

# Function to simulate a sale
def process_sale(product, quantity):
    if product in inventory and inventory[product] >= quantity:
        inventory[product] -= quantity
        print(f"Sold {quantity} {product}. Remaining stock: {inventory[product]}")
    else:
        print(f"Not enough inventory for {product}.")

# Function to add stock
def add_stock(product, quantity):
    if product in inventory:
        inventory[product] += quantity
        print(f"Added {quantity} {product}. New stock: {inventory[product]}")
    else:
        print(f"Product {product} not found in inventory.")

# Simulate transactions
process_sale("laptops", 5)
add_stock("smartphones", 10)

# Displaying updated inventory using dynamic views
print("\nUpdated Inventory:")
for product, quantity in inventory_items:
    print(f"{product}: {quantity}")
```

Explanation

- Inventory Management: The inventory dictionary keeps track of stock quantities for different products.

- Dynamic Views: The inventory_keys, inventory_values, and inventory_items variables are dynamic views on the dictionary's keys, values, and key-value pairs. Any changes to the inventory dictionary (like sales or stock additions) are automatically reflected in these views.
- Sales and Stock Addition: Functions process_sale and add_stock modify the inventory dictionary to reflect sales and restocking, respectively.

Benefits of Dynamic Views
- Real-Time Synchronization: Since views are dynamically linked to the dictionary, any changes made to the dictionary are instantly visible in the views without additional operations or updates.
- Memory Efficiency: Dynamic views do not create new copies of the data; they provide a window into the original dictionary, making them memory efficient.
- Flexibility: Useful for scenarios where the dictionary is being updated based on real-world events (e.g., sales, stock updates) and you need to continuously monitor or display the current state of data.

Conclusion
This example illustrates how dynamic views on a dictionary can be effectively used in a real-world application such as inventory management. By leveraging the real-time synchronization of views with the underlying dictionary, developers can create efficient and responsive systems that automatically reflect changes in data structures, enhancing both performance and usability.

Example 2.14
GUI Tkinter for Real-Time Inventory Tracking System
To build a rich graphical user interface (GUI) in Tkinter that simulates inventory management with real-time interactions such as processing sales and adding stock, we will develop a Python class-based application. This GUI will allow users to interactively manage product inventories, reflecting changes immediately.

Step 1: Define the GUI Class for Inventory Management
We will define a main class for our GUI, which will handle initializing the main window and provide methods for managing the inventory.

```python
import tkinter as tk
from tkinter import ttk, messagebox, simpledialog

class InventoryManagerApp:
    def __init__(self, master):
        self.master = master
        self.master.title("Inventory Manager")
        self.master.geometry("400x300")

        # Initialize the inventory
        self.inventory = {
            "laptops": 30,
            "smartphones": 50,
            "tablets": 20
        }

        # GUI Setup
        self.setup_widgets()

    def setup_widgets(self):
        # Label for instruction
        ttk.Label(self.master, text="Manage Inventory", font=('Arial', 16)).pack(pady=10)

        # Buttons for managing inventory
        ttk.Button(self.master, text="Process Sale", command=self.process_sale).pack(pady=5)
        ttk.Button(self.master, text="Add Stock", command=self.add_stock).pack(pady=5)
        ttk.Button(self.master, text="Show Inventory", command=self.show_inventory).pack(pady=5)

        # Text box to display inventory or results
        self.text_display = tk.Text(self.master, height=10, width=40)
        self.text_display.pack(pady=20)

    def process_sale(self):
        product = simpledialog.askstring("Process Sale", "Enter product name:")
        quantity = simpledialog.askinteger("Process Sale", "Enter quantity:")
        if product in self.inventory and self.inventory[product] >= quantity:
            self.inventory[product] -= quantity
            messagebox.showinfo("Sale Processed", f"Sold {quantity} {product}. Remaining stock: {self.inventory[product]}")
        else:
            messagebox.showerror("Error", f"Not enough inventory for {product}.")
        self.show_inventory()

    def add_stock(self):
        product = simpledialog.askstring("Add Stock", "Enter product name:")
        quantity = simpledialog.askinteger("Add Stock", "Enter quantity:")
        if product in self.inventory:
```

```
            self.inventory[product] += quantity
            messagebox.showinfo("Stock Added", f"Added {quantity} {product}. New stock: {self.inventory[product]}")
        else:
            messagebox.showerror("Error", f"Product {product} not found in inventory.")
        self.show_inventory()

    def show_inventory(self):
        self.text_display.delete('1.0', tk.END)
        self.text_display.insert(tk.END, "Current Inventory:\n")
        for product, quantity in self.inventory.items():
            self.text_display.insert(tk.END, f"{product}: {quantity}\n")

if __name__ == "__main__":
    root = tk.Tk()
    app = InventoryManagerApp(root)
    root.mainloop()
```

Explanation of the Code

1. Class Definition (InventoryManagerApp):
   Initializes the main window (master) and sets up GUI components for interacting with inventory data, allowing for the processing of sales, addition of stock, and viewing inventory updates.
2. Widget Setup (setup_widgets):
   Configures the GUI layout with buttons for inventory management actions and a text display for showing inventory or transaction results.
3. Interactive Inventory Management:
   - process_sale and add_stock allow the user to interactively manage inventory by entering product names and quantities through dialog prompts. Changes are reflected immediately and validated with feedback via message boxes.
   - show_inventory updates the text display widget with the current state of the inventory.

Features of the GUI

- Dynamic User Interaction: Users can dynamically process sales and add stock, with each action immediately updating the inventory.
- Real-Time Feedback: The GUI provides instant feedback on the effects of user actions, enhancing usability and ensuring accurate inventory management.

- Clear and User-Friendly Interface: The straightforward design with clear instructions and immediate error handling makes inventory management accessible and efficient.

This GUI application effectively demonstrates how a graphical interface can enhance interaction with inventory data, making management tasks more intuitive and responsive.

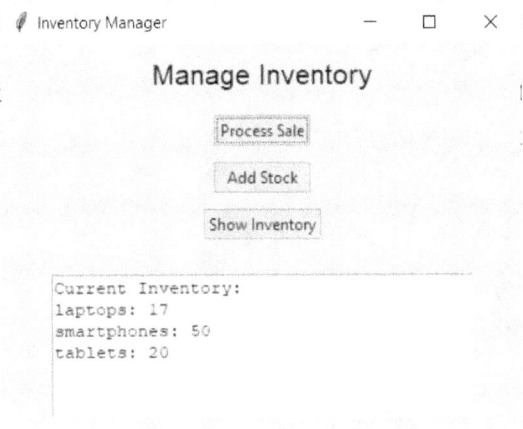

Example 2.15
Implementing a Role-Based Access Control (RBAC) System
Dictionary membership testing in Python is a powerful feature that allows you to quickly check if a key exists in a dictionary. This is extremely useful in many real-world scenarios, particularly where you need to validate the presence of an identifier, setting, or any other unique element within a data structure before proceeding with additional operations.

Let's take a practical example where dictionary membership testing is vital: a Role-Based Access Control (RBAC) system in a software application. In this system, different users have different roles, and each role has specific permissions. We can use dictionaries to map roles to their permissions and efficiently check whether a role has the right to perform a certain action.

Setup RBAC Structure and Functions
Here's how you might implement basic RBAC features using dictionaries:

```
# Dictionary to hold roles and their respective permissions
permissions = {
```

```
    "admin": {"edit", "delete", "view"},
    "editor": {"edit", "view"},
    "viewer": {"view"}
}

# Function to check if a role has a specific permission
def has_permission(role, action):
    if role in permissions:
        if action in permissions[role]:
            return True
        else:
            return False
    else:
        raise ValueError("Role does not exist")

# Example usage to check permissions
try:
    role = "editor"
    action = "delete"
    if has_permission(role, action):
        print(f"The role {role} has permission to {action}.")
    else:
        print(f"The role {role} does not have permission to {action}.")
except ValueError as e:
    print(e)

# Another example checking if a role has a permission
role = "viewer"
action = "view"
if has_permission(role, action):
    print(f"The role {role} has permission to {action}.")
else:
    print(f"The role {role} does not have permission to {action}.")
```

Explanation

- RBAC Data Structure: The permissions dictionary maps roles (like "admin", "editor", and "viewer") to a set of actions they are allowed to perform ("edit", "delete", "view").
- Membership Testing: The function has_permission first checks if the role exists in the permissions dictionary. This membership test (if role in permissions:) is crucial to ensure that the function handles only defined roles and throws an error for undefined roles.
- Action Permission Check: Once the role is confirmed to exist, the function checks if the specified action is in the set of permissions associated with that role. This quickly confirms whether the role is allowed to perform the action.

Benefits of Dictionary Membership Testing
- Efficiency: Membership tests in dictionaries are fast because dictionaries in Python are implemented using hash tables.
- Clarity: The operation key in dict is both readable and straightforward, making the code easy to understand.
- Safety: Checking for membership before accessing a dictionary key helps prevent runtime errors, such as KeyError.

Conclusion
This example shows how dictionary membership testing is an integral part of implementing a secure and efficient Role-Based Access Control system in software applications. By utilizing dictionaries for both roles and permissions, you can achieve quick checks and validations, ensuring that operations proceed only if the appropriate permissions are present. This not only enhances security but also improves the performance and reliability of the application.

Example 2.16
GUI Tkinter for Implementing a Role-Based Access Control (RBAC) System
To create a rich graphical user interface (GUI) using Tkinter that interacts with a system for managing user roles and permissions, we will build a Python class-based application. This GUI will allow users to check if a specific role has the necessary permissions for certain actions, updating the interface in real-time based on user input.

Step 1: Define the GUI Class for Role and Permission Management
The main class will manage the initialization of the GUI window and provide methods for user interaction to verify role permissions.

```python
import tkinter as tk
from tkinter import ttk, messagebox, simpledialog

class PermissionManagerApp:
    def __init__(self, master):
        self.master = master
        self.master.title("Permission Manager")
        self.master.geometry("500x300")
```

```python
        # Initialize permissions dictionary
        self.permissions = {
            "admin": {"edit", "delete", "view"},
            "editor": {"edit", "view"},
            "viewer": {"view"}
        }

        # Setup GUI
        self.setup_widgets()

    def setup_widgets(self):
        # Label for instructions
        ttk.Label(self.master, text="Check Role Permissions", font=('Arial', 16)).pack(pady=10)

        # Entry for role
        ttk.Label(self.master, text="Role:").pack()
        self.role_entry = ttk.Entry(self.master, width=20)
        self.role_entry.pack(pady=5)

        # Entry for action
        ttk.Label(self.master, text="Action:").pack()
        self.action_entry = ttk.Entry(self.master, width=20)
        self.action_entry.pack(pady=5)

        # Button to check permission
        ttk.Button(self.master, text="Check Permission", command=self.check_permission).pack(pady=10)

        # Label to display result
        self.result_label = ttk.Label(self.master, text="", font=('Arial', 12))
        self.result_label.pack(pady=20)

    def check_permission(self):
        role = self.role_entry.get().strip()
        action = self.action_entry.get().strip()
        try:
            if self.has_permission(role, action):
                self.result_label.config(text=f"The role {role} has permission to {action}.", foreground='green')
            else:
                self.result_label.config(text=f"The role {role} does not have permission to {action}.", foreground='red')
        except ValueError as e:
            messagebox.showerror("Error", str(e))

    def has_permission(self, role, action):
        if role in self.permissions:
            if action in self.permissions[role]:
                return True
```

```
            else:
                return False
        else:
            raise ValueError("Role does not exist")

if __name__ == "__main__":
    root = tk.Tk()
    app = PermissionManagerApp(root)
    root.mainloop()
```

Check Role Permissions

Role: admin
Action: edit

[Check Permission]

The role admin has permission to edit.

Explanation of the Code

1. Class Definition (PermissionManagerApp):
   Initializes the main window (master) and sets up GUI components for interacting with role permissions, including entries for role and action and a button to verify permissions.
2. Widget Setup (setup_widgets):
   Configures the GUI layout, adding entry fields for the role and action, a button to initiate the permission check, and a label to display results.
3. Permission Verification (check_permission):
   Retrieves the user input for role and action, checks permissions using the has_permission method, and updates the label to display whether the role has the requested permission or an error if the role does not exist.

Features of the GUI

- Interactive Data Input: Users can enter a role and an action to dynamically check for permissions.

- Real-Time Feedback: Provides immediate feedback on whether the specified role has the necessary permission, enhancing user interaction.
- Error Handling: Displays error messages for non-existent roles, ensuring the user is informed of incorrect inputs.

This GUI application provides an intuitive and efficient way to manage and verify user role permissions within a system, making it a practical tool for administrators or users in any system that requires role-based access control.

Example 2.17
Merging Customer Data from Multiple Sources

In Python, the update() method of dictionaries is commonly used to merge two dictionaries or to update a dictionary with key-value pairs from another dictionary, iterable, or keyword arguments. This is particularly useful in scenarios where you need to combine data from different sources or when you want to modify or extend the existing dictionary entries based on new or incoming data.

Consider a scenario in an e-commerce business where customer data is collected from multiple sources. For instance, the basic customer data might be collected at registration, and additional preferences or details could be gathered from subsequent interactions or surveys. The update() method can be used effectively to merge these data points into a unified customer profile.

Setup Customer Profile and Update Mechanism
Here's how you might manage and update customer profiles using the update() method:

```
# Dictionary holding initial customer data
customer_profiles = {
    "001": {"name": "Alice Johnson", "email": "alice@example.com"},
    "002": {"name": "Bob Smith", "email": "bob@example.com"}
}

# Additional data collected from a follow-up survey
survey_data = {
    "001": {"favorite_color": "blue", "newsletter_subscribed": True},
    "002": {"favorite_color": "green", "newsletter_subscribed": False}
}

# Function to update customer profiles with survey data
def update_customer_profiles(customers, updates):
```

```
    for customer_id, data in updates.items():
        if customer_id in customers:
            customers[customer_id].update(data)
            print(f"Updated profile for {customer_id}: {customers[customer_id]}")
        else:
            print(f"No existing profile found for customer ID {customer_id}.")

# Example usage
update_customer_profiles(customer_profiles, survey_data)

# Output:
# Updated profile for 001: {'name': 'Alice Johnson', 'email': 'alice@example.com',
'favorite_color': 'blue', 'newsletter_subscribed': True}
# Updated profile for 002: {'name': 'Bob Smith', 'email': 'bob@example.com',
'favorite_color': 'green', 'newsletter_subscribed': False}
```

Explanation

- Initial and Additional Data: The customer_profiles dictionary contains initial data for customers, while survey_data contains additional preferences collected later.
- Using update(): The function update_customer_profiles takes the existing dictionary of customer profiles and an updates dictionary. It iterates through the updates, and for each customer, it uses update() to merge the additional data into the existing profiles.

This approach is beneficial because:

- Efficiency: The update() method provides a quick and easy way to merge two dictionaries, especially useful when dealing with larger datasets or needing frequent updates.
- Maintainability: By separating the logic for updating profiles into a function, the code becomes easier to maintain and extend, for instance, adding error checking or handling new types of updates.
- Flexibility: It allows for dynamic updates to the data structure, accommodating changes in the information structure without significant modifications to the codebase.

Conclusion

This example illustrates how the update() method can be used to effectively manage and synchronize customer data in real-world applications. By merging dictionaries in this way, developers can ensure that their applications remain flexible and efficient, particularly in scenarios involving dynamic data updates. The method simplifies the process of integrating multiple data sources, enhancing the ability to maintain comprehensive and up-to-date user profiles or other similar datasets.

Example 2.18
GUI Tkinter for Merging Customer Data from Multiple Sources

To create a rich graphical user interface (GUI) using Tkinter that integrates and updates customer profiles with additional survey data, we can build a Python class-based application. This GUI will allow users to view updated customer profiles and interactively apply updates from survey data.

Step 1: Define the GUI Class for Customer Data Integration

We'll define the main class for our GUI, which will manage the initialization of the main window and provide methods for displaying and updating customer data.

```
import tkinter as tk
from tkinter import ttk, messagebox

class CustomerDataApp:
    def __init__(self, master):
        self.master = master
        self.master.title("Customer Data Integration")
        self.master.geometry("500x400")

        # Initialize customer and survey data
        self.customer_profiles = {
            "001": {"name": "Alice Johnson", "email": "alice@example.com"},
            "002": {"name": "Bob Smith", "email": "bob@example.com"}
        }
        self.survey_data = {
            "001": {"favorite_color": "blue", "newsletter_subscribed": True},
            "002": {"favorite_color": "green", "newsletter_subscribed": False}
        }

        # GUI Setup
        self.setup_widgets()

    def setup_widgets(self):
        # Button to update customer profiles
        ttk.Button(self.master,              text="Update           Profiles", command=self.update_profiles).pack(pady=20)

        # Text box to display profiles
```

```python
        self.text_display = tk.Text(self.master, height=15, width=50)
        self.text_display.pack(pady=20)

        # Initially display current profiles
        self.display_profiles()

    def update_profiles(self):
        # Update profiles with survey data
        self.update_customer_profiles(self.customer_profiles, self.survey_data)
        self.display_profiles()
        messagebox.showinfo("Update Successful", "Customer profiles have been updated.")

    def display_profiles(self):
        # Display updated profiles in the text widget
        self.text_display.delete('1.0', tk.END)
        for customer_id, profile in self.customer_profiles.items():
            profile_text = f"ID {customer_id}: {profile}\n"
            self.text_display.insert(tk.END, profile_text)

    def update_customer_profiles(self, customers, updates):
        # Update each customer profile with additional data
        for customer_id, data in updates.items():
            if customer_id in customers:
                customers[customer_id].update(data)
                print(f"Updated profile for {customer_id}: {customers[customer_id]}")

if __name__ == "__main__":
    root = tk.Tk()
    app = CustomerDataApp(root)
    root.mainloop()
```

Explanation of the Code

1. Class Definition (CustomerDataApp):

   Initializes the main window and sets up GUI components to interact with and display updated customer profiles.

2. Widget Setup (setup_widgets):

   Configures the GUI layout, adding a button to trigger the update of customer profiles with survey data and a text display area to show the customer profiles.

3. Profile Updates and Display:

   - update_profiles triggers the update of customer profiles with the survey data, refreshes the display, and confirms the successful update via a messagebox.
   - display_profiles updates the text display widget to show the current state of the customer profiles, reflecting any updates.

4. Updating Customer Profiles (update_customer_profiles):
   Merges survey data into existing customer profiles, ensuring the data is integrated and updated appropriately.

Features of the GUI
- Interactive Data Management: The GUI allows users to update customer profiles dynamically with additional data and view the results in real-time.
- Immediate Feedback: Provides immediate visual feedback on customer data updates, enhancing usability.
- Clear and User-Friendly Interface: The straightforward layout with clear instructions and immediate feedback makes the application accessible and easy to use.

This GUI application provides a practical demonstration of how a graphical interface can enhance interaction with complex data sets, making the integration and management of customer information more efficient and user-friendly.

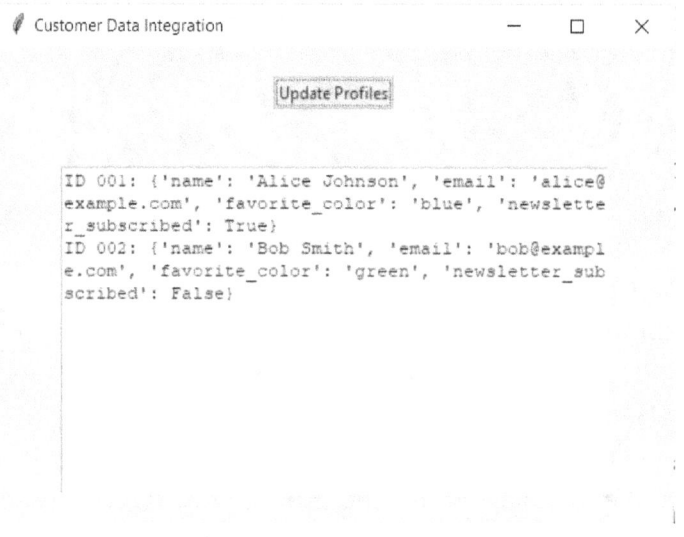

Example 2.19
Setting Up a Voting System
The fromkeys() method in Python is a class method for dictionaries that creates a new dictionary with keys from a given iterable and values set to a specified value. This method is particularly useful when you need to initialize a dictionary with a specific set of keys, each with the same default value. This can simplify setup processes in many applications, such as initializing settings, tracking state, or preparing data structures for processing.

Let's consider a scenario where fromkeys() can be used effectively: setting up a voting system for a small organization's election. In this system, each member of the organization is allowed to vote once in an election, and the system needs to track whether each member has voted.

Setup Member Voting Status
Here's how you might implement this using the fromkeys() method:

```python
# List of members eligible to vote
members = ["Alice", "Bob", "Charlie", "Dana", "Eli"]

# Creating a dictionary to track voting status
voting_status = dict.fromkeys(members, False)

print("Initial Voting Status:")
print(voting_status)

# Function to record a vote
def cast_vote(member_name):
    if member_name in voting_status and not voting_status[member_name]:
        voting_status[member_name] = True
        print(f"Vote cast for {member_name}.")
    elif member_name in voting_status and voting_status[member_name]:
        print(f"{member_name} has already voted. No duplicate votes allowed.")
    else:
        print(f"{member_name} is not a recognized member.")

# Example of members voting
cast_vote("Alice")
cast_vote("Bob")
cast_vote("Alice")  # Trying to vote again

print("\nUpdated Voting Status:")
print(voting_status)

# Output:
```

```
# Initial Voting Status:
# {'Alice': False, 'Bob': False, 'Charlie': False, 'Dana': False, 'Eli': False}
# Vote cast for Alice.
# Vote cast for Bob.
# Alice has already voted. No duplicate votes allowed.
#
# Updated Voting Status:
# {'Alice': True, 'Bob': True, 'Charlie': False, 'Dana': False, 'Eli': False}
```

Explanation

- Member List and Voting Dictionary: The members list contains the names of all members eligible to vote. The voting_status dictionary is initialized using fromkeys(), setting the default voting status of each member to False indicating they have not yet voted.
- Casting a Vote: The cast_vote function checks the member's current voting status. If they haven't voted, their status is updated to True. If they have already voted, it prevents them from voting again.
- Safety and Control: The system ensures that each member can only vote once and that only valid members can cast a vote.

Benefits of fromkeys()

- Efficiency: The fromkeys() method allows for quick initialization of a dictionary with a default value for each key, which is much faster and more readable than looping through an iterable manually.
- Simplicity: It simplifies the creation of a dictionary when all keys need to start with the same value, making the code cleaner and easier to understand.

Conclusion

This example demonstrates how fromkeys() can be effectively used in practical applications like setting up a voting system where initial states need to be uniformly set. The method provides a straightforward way to initialize dictionaries, ensuring that the system starts in a consistent state, ready for processing subsequent actions. This use case can be adapted to various scenarios where initial state setup is crucial, from tracking usage rights in software to initializing game boards in digital board games.

Example 2.20
GUI Tkinter for Setting Up a Voting System
To create an advanced graphical user interface (GUI) in Tkinter that allows real-time interaction with a voting system for members of a community or organization, we will build a Python class-based application. This GUI will allow users to cast votes, prevent duplicate voting, and display the current voting status dynamically.

Step 1: Define the GUI Class for the Voting System
We will define a main class for our GUI that will manage initializing the main window and provide methods for handling user interactions related to voting.

```
import tkinter as tk
from tkinter import ttk, messagebox, simpledialog

class VotingApp:
    def __init__(self, master):
        self.master = master
        self.master.title("Voting System")
        self.master.geometry("400x300")

        # Initialize member list and voting status
        self.members = ["Alice", "Bob", "Charlie", "Dana", "Eli"]
        self.voting_status = dict.fromkeys(self.members, False)

        # GUI Setup
        self.setup_widgets()

    def setup_widgets(self):
        # Label for instructions
        ttk.Label(self.master, text="Click to cast your vote", font=('Arial', 16)).pack(pady=20)

        # Buttons for each member
        for member in self.members:
            button = ttk.Button(self.master, text=f"Vote for {member}",
                                command=lambda m=member: self.cast_vote(m))
            button.pack(pady=5)

        # Text box to display voting results
        self.text_display = tk.Text(self.master, height=8, width=35)
        self.text_display.pack(pady=20)

        # Button to refresh the voting status display
        ttk.Button(self.master, text="Show Voting Status", command=self.display_voting_status).pack(pady=10)
```

```python
    def cast_vote(self, member_name):
        if member_name in self.voting_status and not self.voting_status[member_name]:
            self.voting_status[member_name] = True
            messagebox.showinfo("Vote Cast", f"Vote cast for {member_name}.")
        elif member_name in self.voting_status and self.voting_status[member_name]:
            messagebox.showerror("Voting Error", f"{member_name} has already voted. No duplicate votes allowed.")
        else:
            messagebox.showerror("Voting Error", f"{member_name} is not a recognized member.")
        self.display_voting_status()

    def display_voting_status(self):
        self.text_display.delete('1.0', tk.END)
        self.text_display.insert(tk.END, "Current Voting Status:\n")
        for member, has_voted in self.voting_status.items():
            status = "Voted" if has_voted else "Not Voted"
            self.text_display.insert(tk.END, f"{member}: {status}\n")

if __name__ == "__main__":
    root = tk.Tk()
    app = VotingApp(root)
    root.mainloop()
```

Explanation of the Code

1. Class Definition (VotingApp):

   Initializes the main window (master) and sets up GUI components for interacting with the voting system, including buttons for each member and a text display area for voting status.

2. Widget Setup (setup_widgets):

   Configures the GUI layout, adding individual voting buttons for each member and a general button to refresh and display the voting status. This setup provides clear and direct interaction for voting.

3. Voting and Display Functions (cast_vote and display_voting_status):

   - cast_vote checks if the selected member has already voted to prevent duplicates and updates the vote status accordingly, with immediate feedback via message boxes.
   - display_voting_status updates the text display widget to show the current voting status of all members, reflecting any changes in real-time.

Features of the GUI
- Interactive Voting: Users can cast votes for each member directly through the GUI, with each button corresponding to a member.
- Dynamic Feedback: Provides immediate visual and informative feedback on the actions taken (e.g., voting, errors), enhancing user interaction.
- Real-Time Updates: Displays up-to-date voting status after each interaction, ensuring the information is current and accurate.

This GUI application demonstrates how to effectively manage and interact with a voting system, providing a user-friendly and efficient way to handle votes and display voting status in real-time for any community or organizational activity.

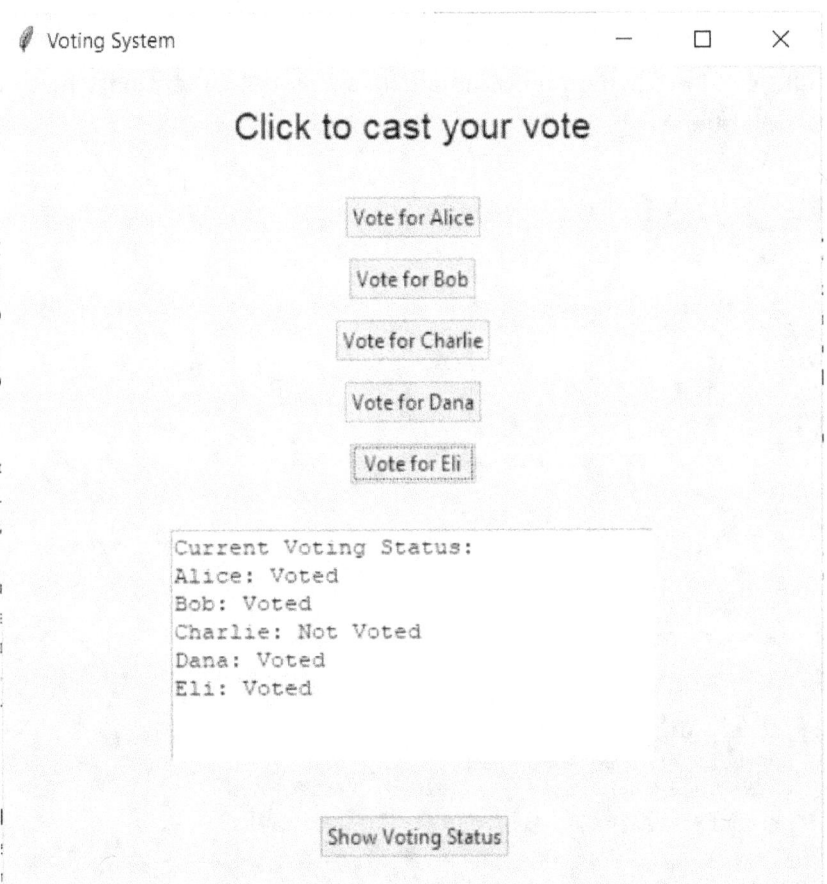

Example 2.21
Sorting a Product Inventory by Sales
Sorting a dictionary in Python is a common task, particularly when you need to present data in a specific order, such as alphabetical or numerical. Python dictionaries are inherently unordered (before Python 3.7, although they maintain insertion order in Python 3.7 and later). However, you can sort them for display or processing purposes using Python's built-in functions.

Imagine you manage an online store, and you have a dictionary that tracks the number of sales per product. You want to sort this dictionary to identify top-selling products or to generate reports where products are listed according to their sales figures.

Setup and Sort the Product Sales Dictionary
Here's an example of how you might implement sorting of a dictionary that maps product names to sales numbers:

```python
# Dictionary containing product sales
product_sales = {
    "Laptop": 150,
    "Smartphone": 450,
    "Tablet": 300,
    "Desktop PC": 200,
    "Headphones": 350,
    "Camera": 225
}

# Sort by sales numbers (ascending order)
sorted_sales_asc = dict(sorted(product_sales.items(), key=lambda item: item[1]))

# Sort by sales numbers (descending order)
sorted_sales_desc = dict(sorted(product_sales.items(), key=lambda item: item[1], reverse=True))

# Display the sorted dictionaries
print("Sales sorted in ascending order:")
for product, sales in sorted_sales_asc.items():
    print(f"{product}: {sales}")

print("\nSales sorted in descending order:")
for product, sales in sorted_sales_desc.items():
    print(f"{product}: {sales}")

# Output:
# Sales sorted in ascending order:
```

```
# Laptop: 150
# Desktop PC: 200
# Camera: 225
# Tablet: 300
# Headphones: 350
# Smartphone: 450
#
# Sales sorted in descending order:
# Smartphone: 450
# Headphones: 350
# Tablet: 300
# Camera: 225
# Desktop PC: 200
# Laptop: 150
```

Explanation
- Data Setup: product_sales holds the number of sales for each product type.
- Sorting Mechanism: The sorted() function is used to sort the dictionary. The items() method returns a view object displaying a list of a dictionary's key-value tuple pairs. The key argument specifies a function of one argument that is used to extract a comparison key from each element in iterable (item[1] for sorting by sales numbers).
- Ascending and Descending Order: By default, sorted() sorts the elements in ascending order. You can reverse this by setting the reverse parameter to True.

Benefits of Sorting Dictionaries
- Improved Readability: Sorted data is often more comprehensible and easier to analyze.
- Data Analysis: Sorting can help in performing data analysis, like identifying top or bottom values.
- Reporting: For reporting purposes, presenting data in a sorted manner (by name, by number, etc.) is generally more useful.

Conclusion

This example shows how sorting a dictionary based on its values (or keys) can be beneficial in real-world scenarios, such as managing inventory or analyzing sales data. Using Python's flexible sorting tools, you can easily prepare dictionaries for reporting, display, or further analysis, tailored to your specific requirements. Whether it's financial records, product catalogs, or user data, sorting dictionaries helps organize and clarify the information you manage.

Example 2.22
GUI Tkinter for Sorting a Product Inventory by Sales
To create a rich graphical user interface (GUI) using Tkinter that displays product sales in both ascending and descending order, and allows for interactive sorting, we will build a Python class-based application. This GUI will enable users to view sorted sales data dynamically and switch between sorting orders based on their preferences.

Step 1: Define the GUI Class for Sales Visualization
We'll define the main class for our GUI, which will manage the initialization of the main window and provide methods for displaying and sorting sales data interactively.

```
import tkinter as tk
from tkinter import ttk

class SalesDataApp:
    def __init__(self, master):
        self.master = master
        self.master.title("Sales Data Visualization")
        self.master.geometry("400x300")

        # Initialize product sales data
        self.product_sales = {
            "Laptop": 150,
            "Smartphone": 450,
            "Tablet": 300,
            "Desktop PC": 200,
            "Headphones": 350,
            "Camera": 225
        }

        # GUI Setup
        self.setup_widgets()

    def setup_widgets(self):
        # Button to sort ascending
        ttk.Button(self.master, text="Sort Ascending", command=self.sort_ascending).pack(pady=5)

        # Button to sort descending
        ttk.Button(self.master, text="Sort Descending", command=self.sort_descending).pack(pady=5)
```

```python
        # Text box to display sorted sales
        self.text_display = tk.Text(self.master, height=12, width=50)
        self.text_display.pack(pady=20)

        # Initially display sales in descending order
        self.sort_descending()

    def sort_ascending(self):
        sorted_sales = dict(sorted(self.product_sales.items(), key=lambda item: item[1]))
        self.display_sales(sorted_sales)

    def sort_descending(self):
        sorted_sales = dict(sorted(self.product_sales.items(), key=lambda item: item[1], reverse=True))
        self.display_sales(sorted_sales)

    def display_sales(self, sorted_sales):
        self.text_display.delete('1.0', tk.END)
        for product, sales in sorted_sales.items():
            self.text_display.insert(tk.END, f"{product}: {sales}\n")

if __name__ == "__main__":
    root = tk.Tk()
    app = SalesDataApp(root)
    root.mainloop()
```

Explanation of the Code

1. Class Definition (SalesDataApp):
   Initializes the main window (master) and sets up GUI components for interactive sorting and displaying of sales data.
2. Widget Setup (setup_widgets):
   Configures the GUI layout, adding buttons for sorting sales data in ascending and descending orders, and a text display area to show the sorted results.
3. Sorting Functions (sort_ascending and sort_descending):
   These functions sort the sales data based on the button clicked, either in ascending or descending order, by applying the sorted function with appropriate lambda functions.
4. Display Function (display_sales):
   Updates the text display widget with sorted sales data, ensuring that the sales information is presented clearly and updated dynamically when a user requests a different sorting order.

Features of the GUI
- Dynamic Sorting: Allows users to dynamically choose and view sales data sorted in ascending or descending order based on their selection.
- Immediate Feedback: Provides instant feedback by updating the displayed sales data immediately after sorting preferences are changed.
- User-Friendly Interface: The straightforward design with clear and specific controls makes it easy for users to interact with the sales data and understand the displayed information.

This GUI application provides a practical demonstration of how a graphical interface can enhance interaction with data, particularly in scenarios requiring dynamic data sorting and visualization, making it a valuable tool for sales analysis or inventory management.

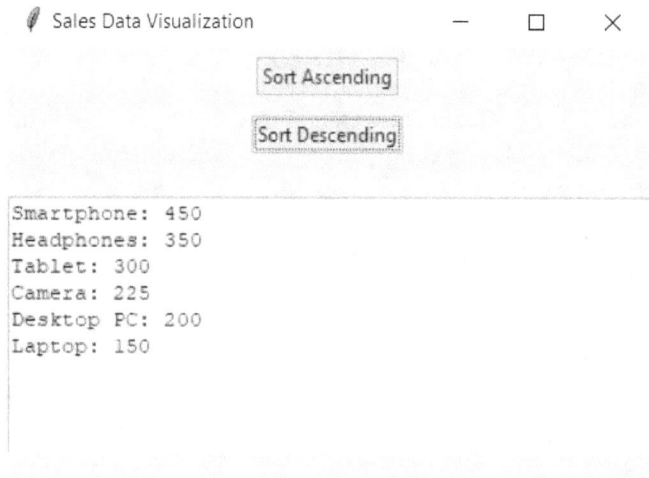

Example 2.23
Sports League Ranking System

Let's delve into a more complex example involving the sorting of a dictionary in a real-world scenario. We will simulate a situation where a sports league needs to sort team statistics based on multiple criteria. This scenario will demonstrate sorting based on a primary criterion and secondary criteria when there are ties.

Imagine you manage a basketball league, and you keep track of each team's statistics in a dictionary. Teams are ranked based on their win percentage, but in case of ties, the secondary criteria are points scored and then points allowed (defensive capability, with fewer points allowed being better).

Data Setup and Sorting Mechanism

Here's how you might implement this sorting system:

```
# Dictionary holding team stats: wins, losses, points scored, points allowed
team_stats = {
    "Lions": {"wins": 10, "losses": 2, "points_scored": 980, "points_allowed": 800},
    "Tigers": {"wins": 8, "losses": 4, "points_scored": 900, "points_allowed": 850},
    "Cheetahs": {"wins": 8, "losses": 4, "points_scored": 920, "points_allowed": 780},
    "Panthers": {"wins": 10, "losses": 2, "points_scored": 950, "points_allowed": 720}
}

# Calculate win percentage and sort by (win percentage, points scored, points allowed)
def calculate_win_percentage(record):
    total_games = record["wins"] + record["losses"]
    return record["wins"] / total_games if total_games > 0 else 0

# Sort teams by win percentage, then by points scored, then by points allowed (ascending)
sorted_teams = sorted(team_stats.items(),
                    key=lambda item: (-calculate_win_percentage(item[1]),
                                      item[1]["points_scored"],
                                      -item[1]["points_allowed"]))

# Display sorted team rankings
print("Team Rankings:")
for rank, (team, stats) in enumerate(sorted_teams, start=1):
    win_percentage = calculate_win_percentage(stats) * 100
    print(f"{rank}. {team} - Win%: {win_percentage:.2f}%, Points Scored: {stats['points_scored']}, Points Allowed: {stats['points_allowed']}")

# Output:
# Team Rankings:
# 1. Panthers - Win%: 83.33%, Points Scored: 950, Points Allowed: 720
# 2. Lions - Win%: 83.33%, Points Scored: 980, Points Allowed: 800
# 3. Cheetahs - Win%: 66.67%, Points Scored: 920, Points Allowed: 780
# 4. Tigers - Win%: 66.67%, Points Scored: 900, Points Allowed: 850
```

Explanation

- Team Statistics: Each team's statistics are stored in team_stats, where each key is a team name and each value is another dictionary containing wins, losses, points scored, and points allowed.

- Sorting Criteria: Teams are sorted first by their win percentage (calculated using the calculate_win_percentage function), then by points scored (more is better), and finally by points allowed (fewer is better).
    - The sorted() function uses a tuple produced by a lambda function to determine the sorting order. Note the use of negative signs for win percentage and points allowed because Python sorts in ascending order by default, but we want the highest values first for these criteria.
- Displaying Results: The sorted results are displayed with a ranking, showing each team's win percentage and points statistics, clearly laid out for league standings.

Benefits of Multi-Criterion Sorting
- Fair and Comprehensive: Using multiple criteria for sorting ensures a fairer ranking system when primary metrics are tied.
- Adaptability: This method can be adapted for various types of data where a nuanced comparison is necessary.
- Complexity Handling: Allows for handling complex scenarios in a straightforward and efficient manner.

Conclusion
This example illustrates how sorting a dictionary on multiple criteria can be implemented to handle complex real-world scenarios effectively. Such sorting mechanisms are especially valuable in sports, business analytics, and any domain where hierarchical data comparison is required for decision-making or reporting. The approach ensures that all important factors are considered, providing a comprehensive and nuanced understanding of the data.

Example 2.24
GUI Tkinter for Sports League Ranking System
To develop a rich graphical user interface (GUI) in Tkinter that displays sports team statistics in a sorted order based on win percentage, points scored, and points allowed, we can create a Python class-based application. This GUI will allow users to view team rankings dynamically, with data sorted according to complex criteria.

Step 1: Define the GUI Class for Sports Team Statistics

The main class will manage the initialization of the GUI window and provide methods for displaying sorted team data.

```python
import tkinter as tk
from tkinter import ttk

class TeamStatsApp:
    def __init__(self, master):
        self.master = master
        self.master.title("Sports Team Rankings")
        self.master.geometry("600x400")

        # Initialize team statistics
        self.team_stats = {
            "Lions": {"wins": 10, "losses": 2, "points_scored": 980, "points_allowed": 800},
            "Tigers": {"wins": 8, "losses": 4, "points_scored": 900, "points_allowed": 850},
            "Cheetahs": {"wins": 8, "losses": 4, "points_scored": 920, "points_allowed": 780},
            "Panthers": {"wins": 10, "losses": 2, "points_scored": 950, "points_allowed": 720}
        }

        # GUI Setup
        self.setup_widgets()

    def setup_widgets(self):
        # Treeview for displaying team rankings
        self.tree = ttk.Treeview(self.master, columns=('Rank', 'Team', 'Win%', 'Points Scored', 'Points Allowed'), show='headings')
        self.tree.heading('Rank', text='Rank')
        self.tree.heading('Team', text='Team')
        self.tree.heading('Win%', text='Win%')
        self.tree.heading('Points Scored', text='Points Scored')
        self.tree.heading('Points Allowed', text='Points Allowed')
        self.tree.pack(fill=tk.BOTH, expand=True, pady=20, padx=20)

        # Initially display sorted team rankings
        self.display_sorted_rankings()

    def calculate_win_percentage(self, record):
        total_games = record["wins"] + record["losses"]
        return record["wins"] / total_games if total_games > 0 else 0

    def display_sorted_rankings(self):
        sorted_teams = sorted(self.team_stats.items(),
                              key=lambda item: (-self.calculate_win_percentage(item[1]),
```

```
                                    item[1]["points_scored"],
                                    -item[1]["points_allowed"]))

        for rank, (team, stats) in enumerate(sorted_teams, start=1):
            win_percentage = self.calculate_win_percentage(stats) * 100
            self.tree.insert('', 'end', values=(rank, team, f"{win_percentage:.2f}%",
stats['points_scored'], stats['points_allowed']))

if __name__ == "__main__":
    root = tk.Tk()
    app = TeamStatsApp(root)
    root.mainloop()
```

Explanation of the Code

1. Class Definition (TeamStatsApp):
   Initializes the main window (master) and sets up GUI components to display team rankings based on calculated statistics.
2. Widget Setup (setup_widgets):
   Configures the GUI layout with a Treeview to display the team rankings. The Treeview shows rankings based on the criteria of win percentage, points scored, and points allowed.
3. Sorting and Display (display_sorted_rankings):
   Sorts the team data by multiple criteria using Python's sorting functions with lambda expressions and displays the results in the Treeview. This method ensures that data is displayed in a structured, easy-to-read format.

Features of the GUI

- Dynamic Data Visualization: The GUI visually represents sports team rankings with detailed statistics in an organized table, making it easy to compare teams based on their performance.
- Interactive and Informative: Users receive comprehensive information about team performance, sorted according to specified criteria.
- Real-Time Updates: While this example does not dynamically update from external data, the GUI is designed to reflect any changes made to the underlying data structure immediately upon re-execution of the sorting function.

This GUI application serves as a robust tool for sports analysts, coaches, or sports enthusiasts to evaluate team performance in a league, providing a clear and efficient way to interpret complex sports data.

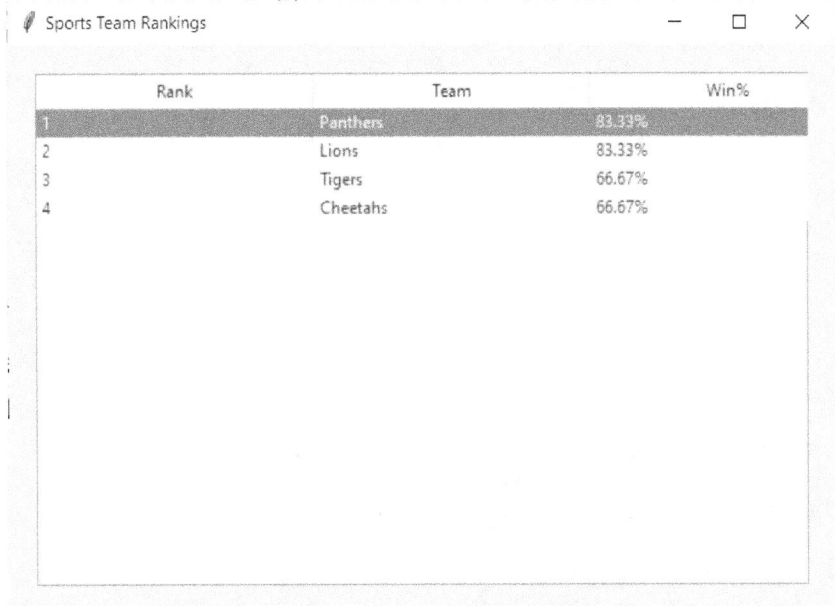

Example 2.25
Using Hashable Objects for Efficient Data Retrieval and Manipulation

In Python, "hashability" is a key concept that determines whether an object can be used as a dictionary key or a set element. To be hashable, an object must have a hash value that does not change during its lifetime and can be compared to other objects. All of Python's immutable built-in objects are hashable, while no mutable containers (like lists or dictionaries) are. However, tuples can be hashable if all their elements are hashable.

Consider a scenario in a healthcare system where each patient is uniquely identified by a combination of several attributes (e.g., first name, last name, and date of birth). These identifiers can be used as keys in a dictionary to quickly access and update patient records.

Setting Up Patient Records Using Tuples as Keys

Here's how you might set up and use a dictionary with hashable keys (tuples) to manage patient records efficiently:

```
# Patient records stored in a dictionary with tuple keys
patient_records = {}

# Tuple of (first_name, last_name, date_of_birth) as a key ensures uniqueness and
immutability
```

```
patient_records[("John", "Doe", "1990-01-01")] = {
    "address": "123 Elm St",
    "phone": "555-1234",
    "email": "johndoe@example.com",
    "medical_history": ["allergy to penicillin", "asthma"]
}

patient_records[("Jane", "Doe", "1992-02-02")] = {
    "address": "456 Oak St",
    "phone": "555-5678",
    "email": "janedoe@example.com",
    "medical_history": ["diabetes"]
}

# Function to retrieve patient information by their identifier
def get_patient_info(first_name, last_name, date_of_birth):
    key = (first_name, last_name, date_of_birth)
    if key in patient_records:
        return patient_records[key]
    else:
        return "Patient record not found."

# Example Usage
info = get_patient_info("John", "Doe", "1990-01-01")
print(info)
info = get_patient_info("Jane", "Doe", "1992-02-02")
print(info)

# Output:
# {'address': '123 Elm St', 'phone': '555-1234', 'email': 'johndoe@example.com', 'medical_history': ['allergy to penicillin', 'asthma']}
# {'address': '456 Oak St', 'phone': '555-5678', 'email': 'janedoe@example.com', 'medical_history': ['diabetes']}
```

Explanation

- Hashable Keys: Each key in the patient_records dictionary is a tuple containing the patient's first name, last name, and date of birth. Since strings are immutable and hashable, and tuples are hashable if all their elements are, these tuples are perfect for use as dictionary keys.
- Efficient Data Retrieval: By using hashable keys that combine multiple data attributes into a single, immutable object, the system can quickly and efficiently retrieve and update patient records. This avoids the complexity and overhead of nested dictionary structures or multiple dictionaries.

Benefits of Using Hashable Objects
- Efficiency: Hash tables (which underpin dictionaries) provide average-case constant-time complexity for lookups, inserts, and deletions, making them extremely efficient for these operations.
- Simplicity: Using a tuple of multiple attributes as a single, hashable key simplifies data structure and data access patterns, compared to more complex hierarchical data structures.
- Flexibility: While maintaining the immutability required for the hashable keys, the values stored in the dictionary can be mutable objects, allowing complex data to be stored and manipulated easily.

Conclusion
This example illustrates the importance of hashability in Python, especially when using complex keys in dictionaries. By understanding and leveraging hashability, you can design more efficient and effective data management solutions in real-world applications, such as this healthcare system scenario. Such practices ensure quick access to data and maintain the integrity and performance of the system.

Example 2.26
GUI Tkinter for Using Hashable Objects for Efficient Data Retrieval and Manipulation
To create a sophisticated real-time graphical user interface (GUI) using Tkinter for managing patient records that are uniquely identified by a tuple of (first_name, last_name, date_of_birth), we will develop a Python class-based application. This GUI will allow users to search for patient information dynamically and display the results interactively.

Step 1: Define the GUI Class for Patient Record Management
The main class will manage the initialization of the GUI window and provide methods for user interaction to retrieve and display patient records based on their unique identifiers.

```
import tkinter as tk
from tkinter import ttk, simpledialog, messagebox

class PatientRecordsApp:
    def __init__(self, master):
        self.master = master
        self.master.title("Patient Records Manager")
        self.master.geometry("600x400")
```

```python
        # Initialize patient records
        self.patient_records = {
            ("John", "Doe", "1990-01-01"): {
                "address": "123 Elm St",
                "phone": "555-1234",
                "email": "johndoe@example.com",
                "medical_history": ["allergy to penicillin", "asthma"]
            },
            ("Jane", "Doe", "1992-02-02"): {
                "address": "456 Oak St",
                "phone": "555-5678",
                "email": "janedoe@example.com",
                "medical_history": ["diabetes"]
            }
        }

        # GUI Setup
        self.setup_widgets()

    def setup_widgets(self):
        # Label for instructions
        ttk.Label(self.master, text="Search Patient Records", font=('Arial', 16)).pack(pady=10)

        # Search button
        ttk.Button(self.master, text="Search Patient", command=self.search_patient).pack(pady=10)

        # Text box to display patient information
        self.text_display = tk.Text(self.master, height=15, width=50)
        self.text_display.pack(pady=20)

    def search_patient(self):
        # Ask user for patient identifiers
        first_name = simpledialog.askstring("Input", "Enter First Name:")
        last_name = simpledialog.askstring("Input", "Enter Last Name:")
        dob = simpledialog.askstring("Input", "Enter Date of Birth (YYYY-MM-DD):")
        info = self.get_patient_info(first_name, last_name, dob)
        self.display_info(info)

    def get_patient_info(self, first_name, last_name, date_of_birth):
        # Retrieve patient information by their identifier
        key = (first_name, last_name, date_of_birth)
        if key in self.patient_records:
            return self.patient_records[key]
        else:
            return "Patient record not found."

    def display_info(self, info):
```

```python
        # Display the patient information or not found message
        self.text_display.delete('1.0', tk.END)
        if isinstance(info, dict):
            for k, v in info.items():
                if isinstance(v, list):
                    v = ", ".join(v)
                self.text_display.insert(tk.END, f"{k.capitalize()}: {v}\n")
        else:
            self.text_display.insert(tk.END, info)

if __name__ == "__main__":
    root = tk.Tk()
    app = PatientRecordsApp(root)
    root.mainloop()
```

Explanation of the Code

1. Class Definition (PatientRecordsApp):
   Initializes the main window and sets up GUI components to interact with patient records.
2. Widget Setup (setup_widgets):
   Configures the GUI layout with a button to initiate a search for patient records and a text display area to show the retrieved patient information or a not found message.
3. Patient Record Search (search_patient):
   Prompts the user to enter the patient's first name, last name, and date of birth, uses these to retrieve patient information, and displays the results.
4. Retrieve and Display Patient Information (get_patient_info and display_info):
   - get_patient_info searches for the patient record based on the unique identifier (tuple of names and date of birth).
   - display_info updates the text display widget with detailed patient information or a not found message if the record does not exist.

Features of the GUI

- Interactive Patient Search: Allows users to dynamically enter patient identifiers to retrieve specific patient records.
- Real-Time Information Display: Updates the display area instantly with patient information, enhancing user interaction.
- User-Friendly Interface: Provides clear instructions and simple input methods, making it easy for users to operate the system.

This GUI application offers a practical demonstration of managing and displaying patient records in a healthcare setting, providing an effective tool for healthcare professionals to access patient information quickly and efficiently.

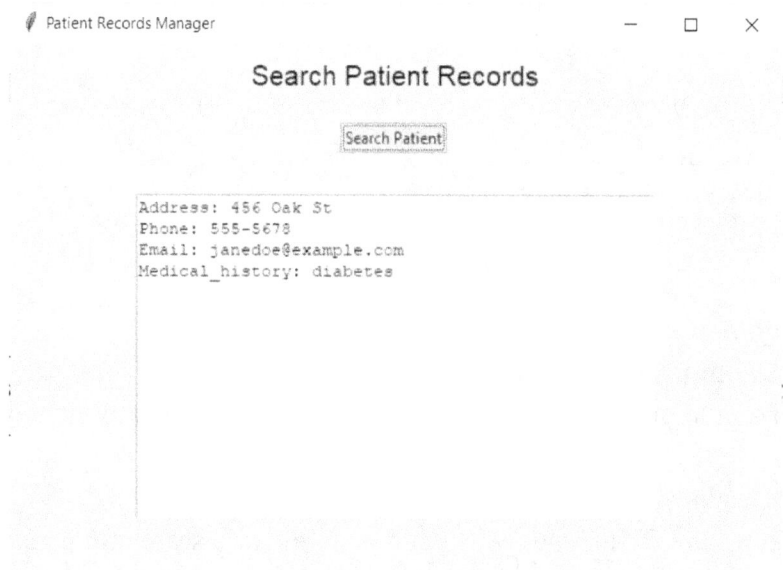

Example 2.27
Caching Function Results with Hashable Inputs
In Python, hashability is a crucial attribute that determines whether an object can be used as a dictionary key or stored in a set. This is because dictionaries and sets in Python are implemented using hash tables, which rely on objects having a hash value that does not change for the lifetime of the object.

A sophisticated application of hashability is in caching function results to optimize performance in cases where function calls are expensive (in terms of computation or time) and are likely to be repeated with the same parameters. This technique, often implemented using decorators in Python, is called memoization.

Imagine you need to convert amounts frequently between various currencies based on the latest exchange rates fetched from an API. Fetching rates frequently can be inefficient and costly, so you decide to cache the results of conversions that have already been computed.

Implementation Using a Memoization Decorator

Here's how you could implement such a caching system:

```python
import functools

# Mock function to simulate fetching exchange rates
def get_exchange_rate(from_currency, to_currency):
    # Imagine this function actually hits a live API
    rates = {
        ('USD', 'EUR'): 0.92,
        ('EUR', 'USD'): 1.09,
        ('USD', 'JPY'): 110.25,
        ('JPY', 'USD'): 0.0091,
    }
    return rates.get((from_currency, to_currency), 1)  # Default to 1 for simplicity

# Memoization decorator to cache results of the convert_currency function
def memoize(func):
    cache = {}
    @functools.wraps(func)
    def memoized_func(*args):
        if args in cache:
            return cache[args]  # Return cached result if available
        result = func(*args)    # Call the function if result not cached
        cache[args] = result    # Cache the result
        return result
    return memoized_func

@memoize
def convert_currency(amount, from_currency, to_currency):
    rate = get_exchange_rate(from_currency, to_currency)
    return amount * rate

# Example usage
print(convert_currency(100, 'USD', 'EUR'))  # Calls the function and caches result
print(convert_currency(100, 'USD', 'EUR'))  # Returns cached result
print(convert_currency(200, 'USD', 'JPY'))  # Calls function and caches new result
```

Explanation

- Hashable Arguments: In the convert_currency function, the arguments amount, from_currency, and to_currency are used. When these arguments are passed to the memoization decorator, they are used as keys in the cache dictionary. Because tuples in Python are hashable if their elements are immutable, the tuple of arguments (amount, from_currency, to_currency) can be used as a dictionary key.
- Function Caching (Memoization): The memoize decorator checks if function arguments have been seen before. If they have, it returns the previously computed

result without re-executing the function, saving time and computational resources. If the arguments haven't been seen, it runs the function, caches the result, and then returns it.
- Performance Improvement: This technique is particularly effective when dealing with repetitive tasks that require expensive computations or API calls. Caching results can significantly improve performance by reducing the number of times these expensive operations need to be performed.

Conclusion
This example illustrates a complex use of hashability in Python to enable caching through a memoization decorator. Using hashable tuples as keys to cache results of function calls based on input arguments showcases how Python's dictionary capabilities can be leveraged to optimize performance in real-world applications, such as financial computations or other scenarios where repeated operations are common. This pattern is particularly useful in improving the efficiency of programs by avoiding unnecessary recalculations.

Example 2.28
GUI Tkinter for Caching Function Results with Hashable Inputs
To create a sophisticated real-time graphical user interface (GUI) using Tkinter that allows users to interactively convert currency values based on live exchange rates, we will develop a Python class-based application. This GUI will enable users to select currencies, input amounts, and instantly view conversion results, taking advantage of caching to optimize performance for repeated queries.

Step 1: Define the GUI Class for Currency Conversion
We'll set up the main class for our GUI, which will manage the initialization of the main window and provide methods for handling currency conversion and displaying results dynamically.

```
import tkinter as tk
from tkinter import ttk, messagebox, simpledialog
import functools

class CurrencyConverterApp:
    def __init__(self, master):
        self.master = master
```

```python
        self.master.title("Currency Converter")
        self.master.geometry("400x300")

        # Exchange rates mockup
        self.rates = {
            ('USD', 'EUR'): 0.92,
            ('EUR', 'USD'): 1.09,
            ('USD', 'JPY'): 110.25,
            ('JPY', 'USD'): 0.0091,
        }

        # GUI Setup
        self.setup_widgets()
        self.setup_memoization()

    def setup_widgets(self):
        # Currency selection
        ttk.Label(self.master, text="From:").pack()
        self.from_currency = ttk.Combobox(self.master, values=list(set(k[0] for k in self.rates.keys())))
        self.from_currency.pack()

        ttk.Label(self.master, text="To:").pack()
        self.to_currency = ttk.Combobox(self.master, values=list(set(k[1] for k in self.rates.keys())))
        self.to_currency.pack()

        ttk.Label(self.master, text="Amount:").pack()
        self.amount_entry = ttk.Entry(self.master)
        self.amount_entry.pack()

        ttk.Button(self.master,                                               text="Convert", command=self.perform_conversion).pack()

        # Result display
        self.result_label = ttk.Label(self.master, text="")
        self.result_label.pack(pady=20)

    def setup_memoization(self):
        self.memo_cache = {}
        self.convert_currency = self.memoize(self.raw_convert_currency)

    def memoize(self, func):
        @functools.wraps(func)
        def memoized_func(*args):
            if args in self.memo_cache:
                return self.memo_cache[args]
            result = func(*args)
            self.memo_cache[args] = result
            return result
```

```
        return memoized_func

    def raw_convert_currency(self, amount, from_currency, to_currency):
        rate = self.get_exchange_rate(from_currency, to_currency)
        return amount * rate

    def get_exchange_rate(self, from_currency, to_currency):
        return self.rates.get((from_currency, to_currency), 1)  # Default to 1 for
simplicity

    def perform_conversion(self):
        amount = float(self.amount_entry.get())
        from_cur = self.from_currency.get()
        to_cur = self.to_currency.get()
        result = self.convert_currency(amount, from_cur, to_cur)
        self.result_label.config(text=f"{amount} {from_cur} = {result:.2f} {to_cur}")

if __name__ == "__main__":
    root = tk.Tk()
    app = CurrencyConverterApp(root)
    root.mainloop()
```

Explanation of the Code
1. Class Definition (CurrencyConverterApp):
   Initializes the main window and sets up GUI components to allow users to select currencies, enter amounts, and view conversion results dynamically.
2. Widget Setup (setup_widgets):
   Configures the GUI with ComboBox widgets for currency selection, an Entry widget for amount input, and a button to trigger the conversion. Results are displayed in a Label widget.
3. Memoization Setup (setup_memoization and memoize):
   Implements a memoization decorator to cache results of currency conversions to enhance performance, particularly for repeated queries.
4. Currency Conversion Functions (raw_convert_currency and get_exchange_rate):
   - raw_convert_currency computes the conversion using live (or mock) exchange rates.
   - get_exchange_rate retrieves the conversion rate from a predefined dictionary, simulating an API response.
5. Performing Conversion (perform_conversion):
   Gathers user input, performs the currency conversion using the memoized function, and updates the GUI to display the results.

Features of the GUI
- Interactive and Dynamic: Users can dynamically select currencies, input values, and convert currencies with results displayed immediately.
- Performance Optimization: Uses memoization to cache results for repeated conversion queries, reducing computational overhead and enhancing response times.
- User-Friendly Interface: Provides a clean, intuitive interface with clear labels, dropdown menus for currency selection, and immediate feedback on operations.

This GUI application showcases a practical implementation of a currency converter that not only provides real-time data interaction but also optimizes performance for frequent operations, making it ideal for financial applications or educational purposes.

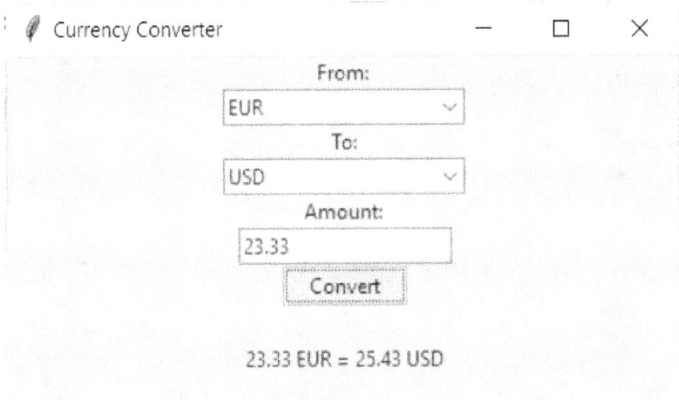

Example 2.29
Shared Configuration Settings

In Python, dictionary aliasing occurs when you assign a dictionary to a new variable, resulting in both variables pointing to the same dictionary object in memory. This means that changes made through one variable are reflected in the other. Understanding and managing aliasing is crucial to avoid unintended side effects in your code, especially when dictionaries are used to store and manipulate shared data across different parts of a program.

Imagine a scenario in a software development project where multiple components of the system share a common configuration dictionary. If one component modifies the configuration, it should be reflected across all components using that configuration. However, if a component needs to make isolated changes without affecting others, proper handling of dictionary aliasing becomes critical.

Scenario Setup and Implementation

Here's an example demonstrating both intentional and unintentional aliasing effects:

```
# Shared configuration for an application
app_config = {
    "debug_mode": False,
    "max_connections": 100,
    "log_path": "/var/log/app.log",
    "user_roles": ["admin", "user", "guest"]
}

# Function to enable debug mode
def enable_debug(config):
    config["debug_mode"] = True

# Function to change log path
def change_log_path(config, new_path):
    config["log_path"] = new_path

# Aliasing: Assigning app_config to new variables for different components
web_server_config = app_config
database_config = app_config

# Enable debug mode using the web_server_config reference
enable_debug(web_server_config)

# Change log path using the database_config reference
change_log_path(database_config, "/var/log/database.log")

# Print the original app_config to see changes
print("app_config:", app_config)

# Trying to isolate changes for a new feature by copying the dictionary
import copy
new_feature_config = copy.deepcopy(app_config)
new_feature_config["max_connections"] = 200

# Print configurations to see the effect
print("web_server_config:", web_server_config)
print("database_config:", database_config)
print("new_feature_config:", new_feature_config)

# Output:
```

```
#   app_config:    {'debug_mode':    True,   'max_connections':    100,   'log_path':
'/var/log/database.log', 'user_roles': ['admin', 'user', 'guest']}
#   web_server_config:   {'debug_mode':   True,   'max_connections':   100,   'log_path':
'/var/log/database.log', 'user_roles': ['admin', 'user', 'guest']}
#   database_config:    {'debug_mode':    True,   'max_connections':    100,   'log_path':
'/var/log/database.log', 'user_roles': ['admin', 'user', 'guest']}
#   new_feature_config:   {'debug_mode':   True,   'max_connections':   200,   'log_path':
'/var/log/database.log', 'user_roles': ['admin', 'user', 'guest']}
```

Explanation

- Dictionary Aliasing: The web_server_config and database_config variables are aliases of app_config. Changes made through these aliases affect the app_config because they reference the same dictionary object.
- Isolating Changes: When creating new_feature_config, a deep copy of app_config is made using copy.deepcopy(). This ensures that changes made to new_feature_config do not affect the original app_config or its aliases. This is crucial when you need to experiment with settings or provide temporary features without affecting global settings.

Key Points

- Intentional Aliasing: Useful when multiple components must remain synchronized with the same configuration settings.
- Unintentional Side Effects: Can lead to bugs if not properly managed, especially when different parts of the system unintentionally affect each other's state.
- Isolation via Copying: Essential for creating independent modifications when needed, using copy or copy.deepcopy() depending on the depth of the dictionary structure.

Conclusion

This example illustrates the importance of understanding dictionary aliasing and its potential impacts on application behavior. Proper management of dictionary references and copies is vital in complex software systems where configurations and state management play a crucial role. The ability to control when and how data is shared or isolated can help maintain robust, predictable software behavior.

Example 2.30
GUI Tkinter for Shared Configuration Settings
To create a sophisticated real-time GUI using Tkinter that interacts with shared application configuration settings, allowing users to modify and observe changes dynamically across different components, we'll develop a Python class-based application. This GUI will illustrate the concept of configuration aliasing and demonstrate how changes to shared configurations propagate unless explicitly copied.

Step 1: Define the GUI Class for Configuration Management
We'll set up the main class for our GUI, which will manage the initialization of the main window and provide methods for adjusting configuration settings interactively.

```
import tkinter as tk
from tkinter import ttk, messagebox, simpledialog
import copy

class ConfigManagerApp:
    def __init__(self, master):
        self.master = master
        self.master.title("Configuration Manager")
        self.master.geometry("500x400")

        # Initialize shared configuration
        self.app_config = {
            "debug_mode": False,
            "max_connections": 100,
            "log_path": "/var/log/app.log",
            "user_roles": ["admin", "user", "guest"]
        }

        # Alias the shared configuration
        self.web_server_config = self.app_config
        self.database_config = self.app_config

        # GUI Setup
        self.setup_widgets()

    def setup_widgets(self):
        # Button to toggle debug mode
        ttk.Button(self.master, text="Toggle Debug Mode", command=self.toggle_debug_mode).pack(pady=10)

        # Button to change log path
        ttk.Button(self.master, text="Change Log Path", command=self.change_log_path).pack(pady=10)
```

```
        # Button to display current config
        ttk.Button(self.master,                   text="Show         Configurations",
command=self.show_configurations).pack(pady=10)

        # Text box to display configurations
        self.text_display = tk.Text(self.master, height=15, width=50)
        self.text_display.pack(pady=20)

    def toggle_debug_mode(self):
        self.app_config["debug_mode"] = not self.app_config["debug_mode"]
        self.show_configurations()

    def change_log_path(self):
        new_path = simpledialog.askstring("Change Log Path", "Enter new log path:")
        if new_path:
            self.app_config["log_path"] = new_path
            self.show_configurations()

    def show_configurations(self):
        configs = (
            f"App Config: {self.app_config}\n"
            f"Web Server Config: {self.web_server_config}\n"
            f"Database Config: {self.database_config}\n"
        )
        self.text_display.delete('1.0', tk.END)
        self.text_display.insert(tk.END, configs)

if __name__ == "__main__":
    root = tk.Tk()
    app = ConfigManagerApp(root)
    root.mainloop()
```

Explanation of the Code
1. Class Definition (ConfigManagerApp):
Initializes the main window and sets up GUI components for interacting with shared configuration settings, including toggling debug mode and changing log paths.
2. Widget Setup (setup_widgets):
Configures the GUI with buttons to toggle debug mode, change the log path, and display current configurations. A text display area is used to show the configuration settings clearly.
3. Configuration Manipulation Methods:
    - toggle_debug_mode switches the debug mode setting in the shared configuration.

- change_log_path allows the user to enter a new log path for the application, which updates the shared configuration.
- show_configurations updates the text display widget to show current configurations, highlighting how changes in one part of the application affect all aliased configurations.

Features of the GUI
- Interactive Configuration Management: Users can modify configurations dynamically and observe how changes in one part of the system affect all configurations due to aliasing.
- Real-Time Updates: The GUI provides immediate feedback on configuration changes, enhancing user interaction and understanding of configuration management.
- Educational Insight: Demonstrates the concept of configuration aliasing and the importance of deep copying when independent changes are necessary.

This GUI application offers a practical demonstration of managing shared application configurations, providing insights into common pitfalls like configuration aliasing and the benefits of using techniques like deep copying to isolate changes in complex systems.

Example 2.31
Web Application Session Management
In complex software development scenarios, understanding and managing dictionary aliasing is crucial to prevent unintended data sharing and modification bugs. Here's a detailed real-world example involving a simulation of user sessions in a web application where dictionary aliasing leads to unintentional side effects. This example will also illustrate how to resolve such issues with deep copying.

Suppose you are developing a web application where user sessions contain mutable user preferences that can be individually customized. If these sessions are improperly aliased, changes intended for one user could inadvertently affect others.

Initial Setup and Problem Illustration
Let's create a basic framework to simulate managing user sessions, where a default session template is used to initialize sessions for new users:

```python
import copy

# Default session settings for new users
default_session = {
    "theme": "light",
    "notifications": {
        "email": True,
        "sms": False
    },
    "language": "English"
}

# Function to create a new user session
def create_user_session(user_id, session_store):
    # Direct aliasing (shallow copy) can cause problems
    session_store[user_id] = default_session.copy()  # Attempt at isolating, but shallow!

# Dictionary to store active user sessions
active_sessions = {}

# Simulate adding sessions for two users
create_user_session("user1", active_sessions)
create_user_session("user2", active_sessions)

# Change theme for user1
active_sessions["user1"]["theme"] = "dark"
```

```
# Change notification preference for user1
active_sessions["user1"]["notifications"]["email"] = False

# Print sessions to see the effects of changes
print("Session for user1:", active_sessions["user1"])
print("Session for user2:", active_sessions["user2"])

# Output:
# Session for user1: {'theme': 'dark', 'notifications': {'email': False, 'sms': False}, 'language': 'English'}
# Session for user2: {'theme': 'light', 'notifications': {'email': False, 'sms': False}, 'language': 'English'}
```

Problem Analysis
- Shallow Copy Issue: The default_session.copy() only creates a shallow copy of the default_session dictionary. While this prevents top-level changes in one user's session from affecting another, nested dictionaries (like notifications) are still shared among all sessions because only the top-level dictionary is copied.

Example 2.32
GUI Tkinter for Web Application Session Management

To create an interactive real-time graphical user interface (GUI) in Tkinter that manages user sessions with customizable settings such as themes, notifications, and language preferences, we will develop a Python class-based application. This GUI will allow users to create new sessions, modify them dynamically, and visually demonstrate the implications of shallow versus deep copying in session management.

Step 1: Define the GUI Class for Session Management

We'll set up the main class for our GUI, which will handle initializing the main window and provide methods for creating and modifying user sessions.

```
import tkinter as tk
from tkinter import ttk, simpledialog, messagebox
import copy

class SessionManagerApp:
    def __init__(self, master):
        self.master = master
        self.master.title("Session Manager")
        self.master.geometry("600x400")

        # Default settings for new user sessions
```

```python
        self.default_session = {
            "theme": "light",
            "notifications": {
                "email": True,
                "sms": False
            },
            "language": "English"
        }

        # Dictionary to store active user sessions
        self.active_sessions = {}

        # GUI Setup
        self.setup_widgets()

    def setup_widgets(self):
        # Buttons to manage sessions
        ttk.Button(self.master, text="Create New Session", command=self.create_new_session).pack(pady=10)
        ttk.Button(self.master, text="Modify Session", command=self.modify_session).pack(pady=10)
        ttk.Button(self.master, text="Show Sessions", command=self.show_sessions).pack(pady=10)

        # Text box to display session information
        self.text_display = tk.Text(self.master, height=15, width=60)
        self.text_display.pack(pady=20)

    def create_new_session(self):
        user_id = simpledialog.askstring("New Session", "Enter user ID:")
        if user_id:
            self.create_user_session(user_id)
            messagebox.showinfo("Session Created", f"Session created for {user_id}.")
            self.show_sessions()

    def create_user_session(self, user_id):
        # Implement deep copy to prevent shared mutable objects
        self.active_sessions[user_id] = copy.deepcopy(self.default_session)

    def modify_session(self):
        user_id = simpledialog.askstring("Modify Session", "Enter user ID to modify:")
        if user_id in self.active_sessions:
            new_theme = simpledialog.askstring("Modify Session", "Enter new theme (light/dark):")
            if new_theme:
                self.active_sessions[user_id]["theme"] = new_theme
            email_notifications = messagebox.askyesno("Modify Session", "Enable email notifications?")
            self.active_sessions[user_id]["notifications"]["email"] = email_notifications
```

```
            self.show_sessions()
        else:
            messagebox.showerror("Error", "Session not found.")

    def show_sessions(self):
        self.text_display.delete('1.0', tk.END)
        for user_id, session in self.active_sessions.items():
            self.text_display.insert(tk.END, f"User {user_id}: {session}\n")

if __name__ == "__main__":
    root = tk.Tk()
    app = SessionManagerApp(root)
    root.mainloop()
```

Explanation of the Code
1. Class Definition (SessionManagerApp):
   Initializes the main window and sets up GUI components to manage user sessions.
2. Widget Setup (setup_widgets):
   Configures the GUI with buttons for creating new sessions, modifying existing sessions, and displaying all session details. A text display area is used for showing session information.
3. Session Management Functions:
   - create_new_session: Prompts the user to enter a user ID and creates a new session using deep copying to ensure that each session is independent.
   - modify_session: Allows the user to modify theme and notification settings for a specified session, demonstrating dynamic changes.
   - show_sessions: Updates the text display widget to show detailed information about all sessions, reflecting any changes in real-time.

Features of the GUI
- Dynamic Session Management: Users can dynamically create, modify, and view sessions, illustrating how user interactions can directly manipulate data structures in a GUI.
- Deep Copy Usage: Demonstrates the importance of using deep copying to avoid unintended shared references in mutable objects, ensuring that changes to one session do not affect others.
- Real-Time Updates and Feedback: Provides instant feedback through message boxes and text display updates, enhancing the user experience and ensuring the GUI remains accurate and informative.

This GUI application provides a practical demonstration of managing session configurations in a system, showcasing the complexities of data handling and the benefits of appropriate copying techniques in software development.

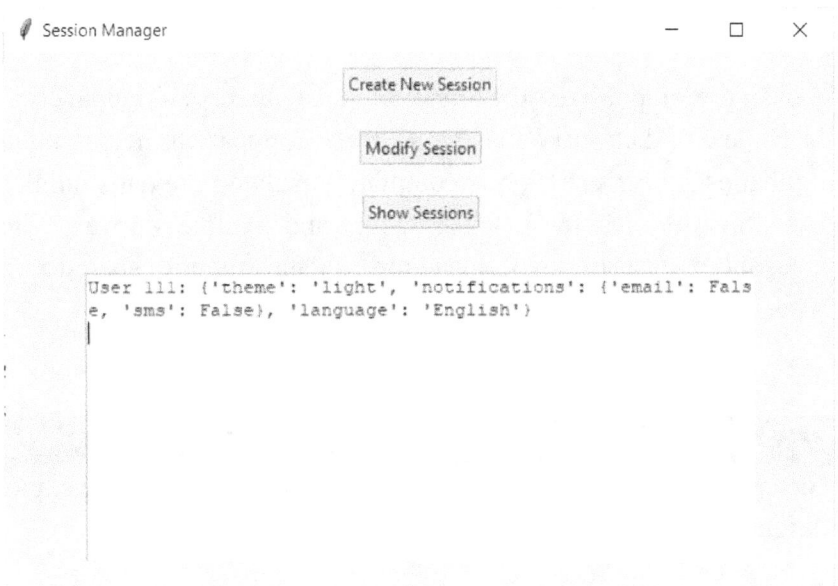

Proper Isolation Using Deep Copy

To fully isolate user sessions, you must use copy.deepcopy() which recursively copies all nested objects:

```
# Function to create a new user session with proper isolation
def create_isolated_user_session(user_id, session_store):
    session_store[user_id] = copy.deepcopy(default_session)

# Reset active sessions and add isolated sessions
active_sessions = {}
create_isolated_user_session("user1", active_sessions)
create_isolated_user_session("user2", active_sessions)

# Make modifications to user1's session again
active_sessions["user1"]["theme"] = "dark"
active_sessions["user1"]["notifications"]["email"] = False

# Now printing the sessions will show that changes to user1 do not affect user2
print("Isolated Session for user1:", active_sessions["user1"])
print("Isolated Session for user2:", active_sessions["user2"])
```

```
# Output:
# Isolated Session for user1: {'theme': 'dark', 'notifications': {'email': False, 'sms':
False}, 'language': 'English'}
# Isolated Session for user2: {'theme': 'light', 'notifications': {'email': True, 'sms':
False}, 'language': 'English'}
```

Conclusion

This refined example emphasizes the importance of understanding deep and shallow copying in the context of dictionary aliasing. For web applications managing user-specific data, ensuring that each user's session is completely isolated prevents unintentional data leakage and modification, leading to more secure and reliable software. This lesson is particularly relevant in scenarios involving complex data structures shared across multiple instances or users.

MORE ADVANCED OPERATIONS

There are a few more nuanced details and advanced topics that could be explored further. Here are additional points and features that might be of interest:

Serialization

JSON Interaction: Python dictionaries are commonly used to represent JSON data. The json module in Python allows you to convert dictionaries to JSON strings and vice versa using json.dumps() and json.loads().

Performance Considerations

Big-O Notation: Operations like looking up keys, adding and removing pairs are generally O(1), i.e., they run in constant time. However, as with any hash table implementation, poor distribution of hash values can degrade to O(n) performance in the worst case.

Advanced Dictionary Uses

- Counter from collections: For tasks that involve counting, Python's collections module has a Counter class that extends dictionaries to automatically count hashable objects.
- DefaultDict for Default Values: collections.defaultdict is another dictionary subclass that calls a factory function to supply missing values, useful for automatic handling of missing keys.

Using dictionaries for Graphs

Dictionaries can represent adjacency lists in graph data structures, helping to model relationships and networks efficiently.

Dict Unpacking

You can unpack dictionaries using the ** operator, useful in function calls where parameters need to be passed as keyword arguments from a dictionary.

Security Considerations

Safe Key Exposure: Be cautious about exposing dictionary keys to untrusted users, as this can reveal internal implementation details.

Contextual Use-Cases

- Dictionaries in Configuration: They are extensively used to store configurations in applications because they allow easy access and straightforward modification.
- Memory Usage: Dictionaries use a significant amount of memory due to their underlying hash table structure, which might be a consideration when handling large data sets.

Decorators and Context Managers

Dictionaries are often used in the implementation of decorators and context managers where function metadata, state, or other attributes need to be stored.

Debugging and Logging

Dictionaries are easy to log or print for debugging due to their clear, readable structure, which makes them particularly useful in development and troubleshooting.

This depth and breadth make dictionaries one of the most versatile and frequently used data structures in Python. Whether you're doing simple tasks or building complex applications, understanding dictionaries will greatly enhance your coding efficiency and capability.

Example 2.33
Word Frequency Analysis in a Document
The Counter from the collections module in Python is a specialized dictionary subclass designed to count hashable objects. It is an extremely useful tool for scenarios involving data analysis, where you need to easily and efficiently count and manipulate occurrences of elements in an iterable.

Suppose you're tasked with analyzing the frequency of words in a document. This could be for a feature in a content management system that highlights commonly used words, assists in SEO (Search Engine Optimization) by identifying key terms, or helps in academic research to identify major themes.

Step-by-Step Implementation
Here's how you could implement a word frequency analyzer using Counter:

```
from collections import Counter
import re

# Sample text for analysis (could be loaded from a file, database, or web scrape)
text = """
Natural language processing (NLP) is a subfield of linguistics, computer science, and
artificial intelligence
concerned with the interactions between computers and human language, in particular
how to program computers to
process and analyze large amounts of natural language data. The result is a computer
capable of understanding the
contents of documents, including the contextual nuances of the language within them.
The technology can then
accurately extract information and insights contained within the documents as well as
categorize and organize the
documents themselves.
"""

# Function to count words
def count_words(text):
    # Use regular expression to find words and convert them to lowercase
    words = re.findall(r'\b\w+\b', text.lower())
    # Create a Counter to count occurrences of each word
    word_counts = Counter(words)
    return word_counts

# Count words in the provided text
word_counts = count_words(text)

# Display the 10 most common words
```

```
print("Most common words:")
for word, count in word_counts.most_common(10):
    print(f"{word}: {count}")

# Output:
# Most common words:
# the: 9
# and: 5
# of: 5
# to: 4
# documents: 4
# language: 3
# computers: 3
# natural: 2
# processing: 2
# within: 2
```

Explanation

- Text Analysis: The sample text is a paragraph about Natural Language Processing. The analysis involves counting the frequency of each word.
- Regular Expression: The re.findall() function is used to find all substrings that match the pattern, which in this case is \b\w+\b—this regex matches sequences of word characters that are whole words.
- Case Normalization: Words are converted to lowercase to ensure that variations in capitalization are not counted as different words.
- Counter Usage: Counter automatically counts how many times each word appears in the list and allows for easy retrieval of the most common words using most_common().

Benefits of Using Counter

- Simplicity: Counter simplifies the code required to count occurrences of items, reducing the need for manual loops and dictionary management.
- Efficiency: Counter is optimized for counting operations, making it faster and more efficient than a general-purpose dictionary for these tasks.
- Functionality: Provides built-in methods like most_common() that further simplify common tasks such as finding the most frequent items.

Conclusion

This example demonstrates how the Counter class from Python's collections module can be leveraged to perform word frequency analysis efficiently and succinctly. This technique is not limited to text analysis and can be adapted for various counting tasks across different domains, such as counting occurrences of specific events in log files, analyzing frequency of items in ecommerce transactions, or even counting biological occurrences in scientific research.

Example 2.34
GUI Tkinter for Word Frequency Analysis in a Document

To create a feature-rich, real-time graphical user interface (GUI) using Tkinter that performs text analysis by counting the frequency of each word in a given text, we will develop a Python class-based application. This GUI will allow users to input their own text, analyze it, and dynamically display the most common words along with their counts.

Step 1: Define the GUI Class for Text Analysis

We'll set up the main class for our GUI, which will handle initializing the main window and provide methods for performing text analysis and displaying results.

```
import tkinter as tk
from tkinter import ttk, scrolledtext
from collections import Counter
import re

class TextAnalyzerApp:
    def __init__(self, master):
        self.master = master
        self.master.title("Text Analyzer")
        self.master.geometry("600x400")

        # GUI Setup
        self.setup_widgets()

    def setup_widgets(self):
        # Text box for user input
        self.input_text = scrolledtext.ScrolledText(self.master, height=10, width=70)
        self.input_text.pack(pady=10)

        # Button to analyze text
        ttk.Button(self.master, text="Analyze Text", command=self.analyze_text).pack(pady=10)
```

```python
        # Text box to display analysis results
        self.result_text = scrolledtext.ScrolledText(self.master, height=10, width=70)
        self.result_text.pack(pady=10)

    def analyze_text(self):
        # Get text from input_text widget
        text = self.input_text.get("1.0", tk.END)
        # Count words in the text
        word_counts = self.count_words(text)
        # Display the 10 most common words
        self.display_word_counts(word_counts)

    def count_words(self, text):
        # Use regular expression to find words and convert them to lowercase
        words = re.findall(r'\b\w+\b', text.lower())
        # Create a Counter to count occurrences of each word
        word_counts = Counter(words)
        return word_counts

    def display_word_counts(self, word_counts):
        # Clear the result text box
        self.result_text.delete("1.0", tk.END)
        # Display the 10 most common words
        self.result_text.insert(tk.END, "Most common words:\n")
        for word, count in word_counts.most_common(10):
            self.result_text.insert(tk.END, f"{word}: {count}\n")

if __name__ == "__main__":
    root = tk.Tk()
    app = TextAnalyzerApp(root)
    root.mainloop()
```

Explanation of the Code

1. Class Definition (TextAnalyzerApp):

    Initializes the main window and sets up GUI components for entering text, analyzing it, and displaying results.

2. Widget Setup (setup_widgets):

    Configures the GUI layout with a scrolled text box for input, a button to trigger analysis, and another scrolled text box for displaying the analysis results.

3. Text Analysis Functions (analyze_text, count_words, display_word_counts):

    - analyze_text: Extracts text from the input widget, counts word occurrences, and displays the results.
    - count_words: Uses regular expressions to find words, converts them to lowercase, and counts their occurrences using Counter.

- display_word_counts: Updates the result text box to show the 10 most common words from the analyzed text.

Features of the GUI
- Interactive Text Input and Analysis: Users can enter text and analyze it on demand, which allows for flexible and immediate text analysis.
- Dynamic Results Display: Provides real-time feedback by displaying the most common words and their counts after each analysis.
- User-Friendly Interface: Offers a clear layout with distinct areas for input, control, and results, making it easy for users to interact with the application.

This GUI application offers a practical tool for text analysis, ideal for educational purposes, preliminary data analysis, or simply exploring text content dynamically.

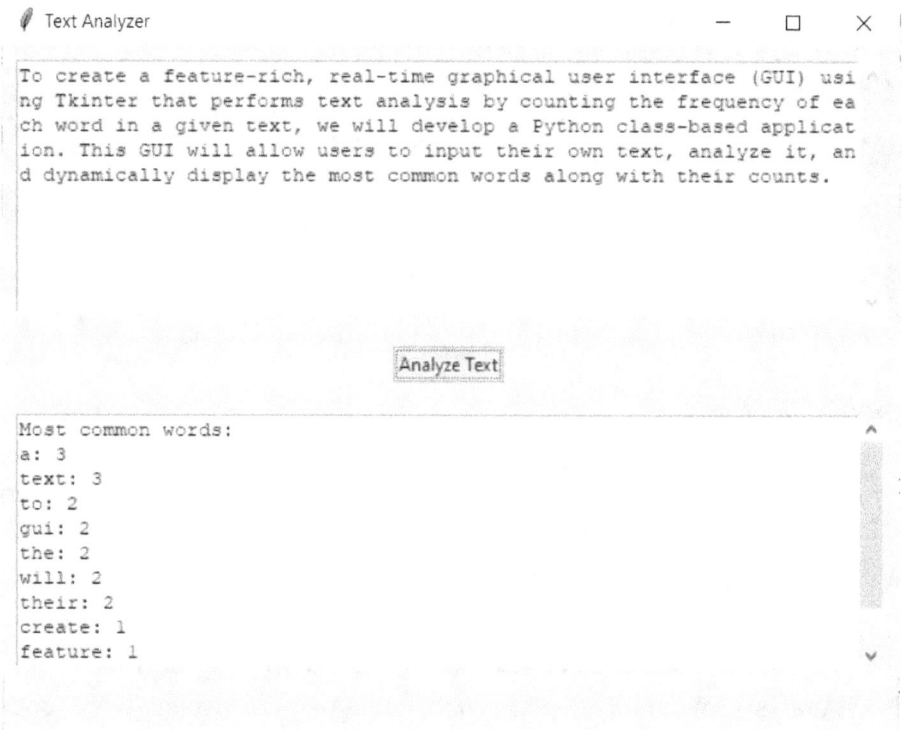

Example 2.35
Ranked-Choice Voting System

Let's delve into a more complex example using Python's Counter from the collections module, where it can be employed in a real-world data analysis scenario involving voting systems and ranked-choice voting (RCV). This example will illustrate how to handle a dataset of ranked votes, count them using Counter, and execute a process to determine the winner in a multi-round voting system.

Ranked-choice voting allows voters to rank multiple candidates in order of preference. If no candidate wins a majority of the first-choice votes, the candidate with the fewest votes is eliminated, and votes for that candidate are redistributed to the next choice listed on each voter's ballot. This process repeats until one candidate has more than half of the active votes.

Scenario Setup

Suppose you are tasked with developing a system to process election results for a local election where ranked-choice voting is used. We will simulate an election with a small number of voters and candidates.

Implementation of the Ranked-Choice Voting System

```
from collections import Counter, defaultdict

# Sample ballots: each list represents a voter's preferences, ranked from most to least
preferred
ballots = [
    ['Alice', 'Bob', 'Charlie'],
    ['Bob', 'Charlie', 'Alice'],
    ['Charlie', 'Alice', 'Bob'],
    ['Alice', 'Charlie', 'Bob'],
    ['Charlie', 'Bob', 'Alice'],
    ['Bob', 'Alice', 'Charlie'],
    ['Alice', 'Bob', 'Charlie'],
    ['Bob', 'Alice', 'Charlie']
]

def count_first_choices(ballots):
    """ Count the first choice votes from each ballot. """
    return Counter(ballot[0] for ballot in ballots)

def ranked_choice_voting(ballots):
    """ Perform a ranked-choice voting tally. """
```

```python
    while True:
        # Count the first choices
        first_choice_counts = count_first_choices(ballots)
        total_votes = sum(first_choice_counts.values())
        print(f"Current counts: {first_choice_counts}")

        # Check if any candidate has more than 50% of the vote
        majority = total_votes / 2
        for candidate, count in first_choice_counts.items():
            if count > majority:
                print(f"Winner: {candidate} with {count} votes")
                return candidate

        # Identify the candidate with the least votes
        least_popular = first_choice_counts.most_common()[-1][0]

        # Remove the least popular candidate and redistribute those votes
        print(f"Eliminating {least_popular} and redistributing their votes.")
        new_ballots = []
        for ballot in ballots:
            new_ballot = [candidate for candidate in ballot if candidate != least_popular]
            new_ballots.append(new_ballot)

        ballots = new_ballots

# Run the election process
ranked_choice_voting(ballots)
```

Explanation

- Ballot Representation: Each voter's preferences are represented as a list of candidates ordered by preference.
- Counting First Choices: The count_first_choices function generates a count of first-choice votes for each candidate using a Counter.
- Majority Check and Redistribution:
    - The election continues until a candidate receives more than half of the total votes.
    - If no candidate achieves a majority, the candidate with the fewest first-choice votes is identified and eliminated.
    - Votes for the eliminated candidate are redistributed to the next preferred candidate on each ballot.
- Iteration: The process repeats until a candidate secures a majority of the active votes.

Benefits of Using Counter
- Efficiency: Counter simplifies counting and can be easily updated or queried, making it perfect for tallying votes.
- Simplicity: Counter operations like most_common() make it easy to identify candidates with the most and least votes.

Conclusion
This complex example showcases how Python's Counter can be effectively utilized in a ranked-choice voting system to handle counting and redistributing votes based on voters' ranked preferences. Such applications are practical in real elections, games, and anywhere decision-making occurs in ranked scenarios.

Example 2.36
GUI Tkinter for Ranked-Choice Voting System
To create an interactive real-time graphical user interface (GUI) using Tkinter that simulates the process of ranked-choice voting, we will build a Python class-based application. This GUI will allow users to input their ballots, run the ranked-choice voting algorithm, and visually observe the elimination and vote redistribution steps until a winner is declared.

Step 1: Define the GUI Class for Ranked-Choice Voting
We will set up the main class for our GUI, which will manage the initialization of the main window and provide methods for inputting ballots, running the voting process, and displaying results.

```
import tkinter as tk
from tkinter import ttk, simpledialog, messagebox
from collections import Counter, defaultdict

class RankedChoiceVotingApp:
    def __init__(self, master):
        self.master = master
        self.master.title("Ranked Choice Voting Simulator")
        self.master.geometry("600x400")

        # Initialize empty list of ballots
        self.ballots = []

        # GUI Setup
```

```python
        self.setup_widgets()

    def setup_widgets(self):
        # Button to add a ballot
        ttk.Button(self.master, text="Add Ballot", command=self.add_ballot).pack(pady=10)

        # Button to start the voting process
        ttk.Button(self.master, text="Start Voting", command=self.start_voting).pack(pady=10)

        # Text box to display voting process and results
        self.text_display = tk.Text(self.master, height=15, width=70)
        self.text_display.pack(pady=20)

    def add_ballot(self):
        """ Prompts the user to enter a ranked ballot. """
        ballot = simpledialog.askstring("New Ballot", "Enter candidates ranked (comma-separated):")
        if ballot:
            self.ballots.append(ballot.split(','))
            messagebox.showinfo("Ballot Added", "Ballot successfully added.")

    def start_voting(self):
        """ Initiates the ranked choice voting process. """
        result = self.ranked_choice_voting(self.ballots)
        messagebox.showinfo("Election Result", f"Winner: {result}")
        self.text_display.insert(tk.END, f"\nWinner: {result}\n")

    def ranked_choice_voting(self, ballots):
        """ Perform a ranked-choice voting tally. """
        self.text_display.delete('1.0', tk.END)
        while True:
            first_choice_counts = self.count_first_choices(ballots)
            total_votes = sum(first_choice_counts.values())
            majority = total_votes / 2
            self.text_display.insert(tk.END, f"Current counts: {first_choice_counts}\n")

            for candidate, count in first_choice_counts.items():
                if count > majority:
                    self.text_display.insert(tk.END, f"Winner: {candidate} with {count} votes\n")
                    return candidate

            least_popular = first_choice_counts.most_common()[-1][0]
            self.text_display.insert(tk.END, f"Eliminating {least_popular} and redistributing votes.\n")
            ballots = [[c for c in ballot if c != least_popular] for ballot in ballots]
```

```
    def count_first_choices(self, ballots):
        """ Count the first choice votes from each ballot. """
        return Counter(ballot[0] for ballot in ballots if ballot)

if __name__ == "__main__":
    root = tk.Tk()
    app = RankedChoiceVotingApp(root)
    root.mainloop()
```

Explanation of the Code

1. Class Definition (RankedChoiceVotingApp):

    Initializes the main window and sets up GUI components for adding ballots, running the election, and displaying results.

2. Widget Setup (setup_widgets):

    Configures the GUI layout with buttons for adding ballots and initiating the voting process. A text display area is used for showing the steps and results of the voting process.

3. Ballot Addition (add_ballot):

    Allows the user to input a ranked list of candidates for a ballot, which is then added to the list of ballots.

4. Voting Process (start_voting and ranked_choice_voting):

    - start_voting triggers the ranked-choice voting algorithm.
    - ranked_choice_voting simulates the election process by counting votes, determining if there's a majority, eliminating the least popular candidate, and redistributing votes until a winner is found.

Features of the GUI

- Dynamic Ballot Input: Users can dynamically enter ballots, providing flexibility in configuring the election.
- Real-Time Voting Simulation: Provides an interactive simulation of the ranked-choice voting process, including vote counting, candidate elimination, and vote redistribution.
- Detailed Feedback: Shows detailed step-by-step changes in the voting process, enhancing transparency and understanding of ranked-choice voting dynamics.

This GUI application provides a practical demonstration of how a ranked-choice voting system works, making it an excellent educational tool for understanding complex voting systems and their implications.

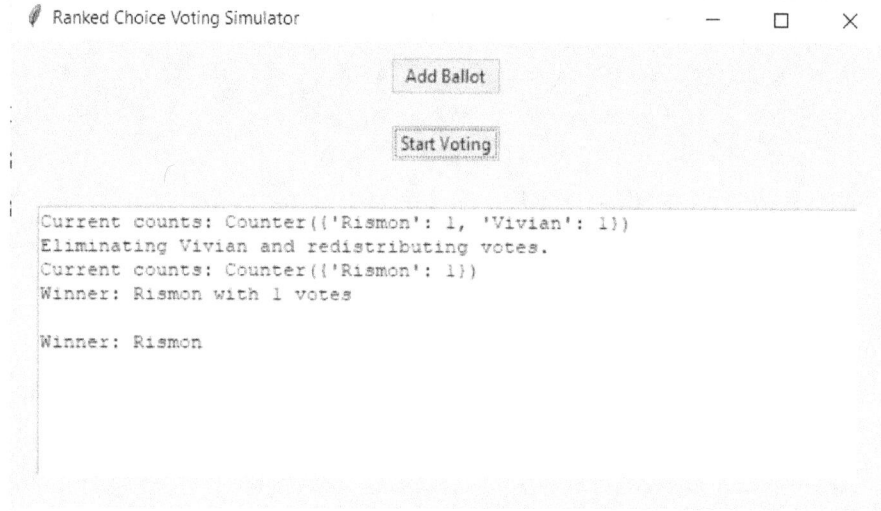

Example 2.37
Network Traffic Monitoring System
Using Python's collections.defaultdict is extremely beneficial when dealing with data that requires a default value for missing keys. This feature of defaultdict allows for more elegant and efficient code, particularly useful in applications involving complex data aggregation, grouping, or categorization without needing to check explicitly for every key's existence.

Imagine you are developing a network monitoring system that tracks the amount of data transferred per protocol over time in a large IT infrastructure. This system needs to aggregate data traffic measurements coming in from various network sensors and update the totals in real-time.

Scenario
The traffic data is categorized by protocol (e.g., HTTP, HTTPS, FTP) and each incoming report (from network sensors) includes the protocol used and the amount of data transferred. The goal is to maintain a running total of data transferred for each protocol.

Implementation Using defaultdict
Here's how you could set up and maintain this monitoring system using defaultdict:

```
from collections import defaultdict
import random
```

```python
# Simulate incoming network traffic data
protocols = ['HTTP', 'HTTPS', 'FTP', 'SSH']
traffic_data = [(random.choice(protocols), random.randint(100, 1000)) for _ in range(100)]

# Defaultdict to store the total data transferred per protocol
traffic_totals = defaultdict(int)  # default factory function is int, which returns 0

def update_traffic(traffic_records):
    """ Update the traffic totals based on incoming records. """
    for protocol, data in traffic_records:
        traffic_totals[protocol] += data

# Simulate updating the system with new batches of traffic data
update_traffic(traffic_data)

# Example usage to display the accumulated traffic data
def display_traffic_totals():
    for protocol, total in traffic_totals.items():
        print(f"Total data for {protocol}: {total} bytes")

display_traffic_totals()
```

Explanation

- Data Generation: Traffic data is simulated as a list of tuples where each tuple represents a single report of data transfer, containing a protocol and the amount of data transferred.
- defaultdict Usage: The traffic_totals dictionary is a defaultdict with int as its default factory. This ensures that any missing protocol key starts with a value of 0 when updated for the first time.
- Data Aggregation: In the update_traffic function, the system iterates over the incoming traffic records and aggregates the data transferred by simply adding the value to the respective protocol in traffic_totals.
- Display Function: The display_traffic_totals function iterates over the traffic_totals dictionary to print out the traffic usage per protocol.

Benefits of Using defaultdict

- Simplicity: Eliminates the need for manual checks or initialization of keys before updating their values, simplifying the code.
- Efficiency: Increases efficiency by reducing the number of lookups in the dictionary; you don't need to check if a key exists before updating its value.

- Versatility: Can be used with different types of factory functions (like list, set, or even custom functions) depending on the needs of the application.

Conclusion

This example demonstrates how defaultdict is ideally suited for applications like real-time data aggregation where keys may not initially exist and where the avoidance of key-checking overhead can lead to more streamlined and performance-efficient code. This approach is particularly valuable in fields such as network monitoring, real-time analytics, and anywhere data must be efficiently categorized and accumulated on-the-fly.

Example 2.38
Tkinter for Network Traffic Monitoring System

To create a sophisticated real-time graphical user interface (GUI) using Tkinter that monitors and displays network traffic data dynamically, we'll develop a Python class-based application. This GUI will visualize traffic data for various network protocols and allow users to simulate the updating of this data, thus providing a practical tool for network administrators or enthusiasts to monitor traffic in a simulated environment.

Step 1: Define the GUI Class for Network Traffic Monitoring

We will set up the main class for our GUI, which will handle initializing the main window and provide methods for simulating traffic data updates and displaying the results.

```python
import tkinter as tk
from tkinter import ttk, messagebox
from collections import defaultdict
import random

class TrafficMonitorApp:
    def __init__(self, master):
        self.master = master
        self.master.title("Network Traffic Monitor")
        self.master.geometry("400x300")

        # Initialize defaultdict to store traffic data per protocol
        self.traffic_totals = defaultdict(int)

        # GUI Setup
        self.setup_widgets()

    def setup_widgets(self):
```

```python
        # Button to simulate traffic data update
        ttk.Button(self.master, text="Update Traffic Data", command=self.update_traffic).pack(pady=10)

        # Text box to display traffic data
        self.text_display = tk.Text(self.master, height=10, width=50)
        self.text_display.pack(pady=20)

        # Initialize display with zero data
        self.display_traffic_totals()

    def update_traffic(self):
        """ Simulate traffic data updates and refresh the display. """
        # Simulate incoming network traffic data
        protocols = ['HTTP', 'HTTPS', 'FTP', 'SSH']
        traffic_data = [(random.choice(protocols), random.randint(100, 1000)) for _ in range(10)]

        # Update the traffic totals
        for protocol, data in traffic_data:
            self.traffic_totals[protocol] += data

        # Display the updated traffic data
        self.display_traffic_totals()

    def display_traffic_totals(self):
        """ Display the accumulated traffic data. """
        self.text_display.delete('1.0', tk.END)
        self.text_display.insert(tk.END, "Traffic Data Totals:\n")
        for protocol, total in self.traffic_totals.items():
            self.text_display.insert(tk.END, f"{protocol}: {total} bytes\n")

if __name__ == "__main__":
    root = tk.Tk()
    app = TrafficMonitorApp(root)
    root.mainloop()
```

Explanation of the Code

1. Class Definition (TrafficMonitorApp):
   Initializes the main window and sets up GUI components for simulating and displaying network traffic data.
2. Widget Setup (setup_widgets):
   Configures the GUI layout with a button to update traffic data and a text display area for showing the current traffic totals for each network protocol.
3. Data Simulation and Display (update_traffic and display_traffic_totals):

- update_traffic: Simulates incoming network traffic data, updates the totals for each protocol, and refreshes the display.
- display_traffic_totals: Updates the text display widget with the latest traffic totals, providing a real-time look at network traffic data.

Features of the GUI
- Interactive Data Simulation: Allows users to simulate incoming network traffic data dynamically with the click of a button, making it ideal for demonstrations or educational purposes.
- Real-Time Data Display: Provides immediate visual feedback on network traffic for various protocols, helping users monitor and analyze network load effectively.
- User-Friendly Interface: Offers a straightforward interface with clear instructions and immediate feedback, making it accessible for users with different levels of technical expertise.

This GUI application provides a practical tool for visualizing and monitoring network traffic data, demonstrating the potential of Tkinter for creating applications that require dynamic data updates and real-time display in network management contexts.

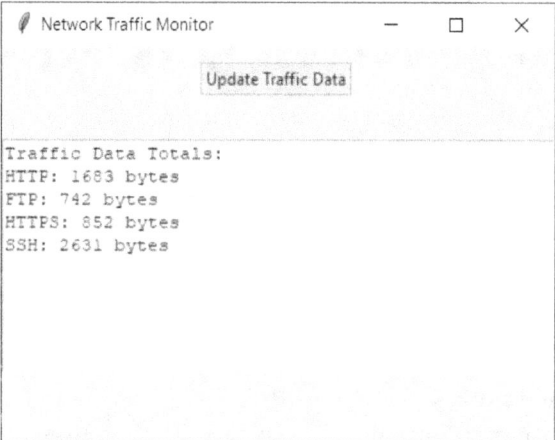

Example 2.39
Building an Inverted Index for Document Search
A complex real-world scenario where collections.defaultdict shines is in natural language processing (NLP), specifically in the construction and manipulation of inverted indices for text search systems. An inverted index is a database index that stores a mapping from content to its locations in a database file, or in this case, documents. This type of index is widely used in document retrieval systems, such as search engines, where it allows fast full-text searches.

Suppose you're tasked with building an inverted index for a set of documents to allow quick retrieval based on word queries. Each entry in the inverted index will list all documents that contain a given word.

Scenario Setup
You have a collection of small text documents, and your task is to build an inverted index using defaultdict so that each word points to a set of document IDs where the word appears.

Implementation Using defaultdict
Here's how you might implement the construction of an inverted index:

```
from collections import defaultdict
import re

# Sample documents dictionary where key is document ID and value is the text
documents = {
    1: "Python is an interpreted high-level general-purpose programming language.",
    2: "Python's design philosophy emphasizes code readability with its notable use of significant whitespace.",
    3: "Its language constructs and object-oriented approach aim to help programmers write clear, logical code for small and large-scale projects.",
    4: "Python supports multiple programming paradigms, including structured (particularly, procedural), object-oriented, and functional programming."
}

# Defaultdict to store the inverted index
inverted_index = defaultdict(set)

def build_inverted_index(docs):
    """ Build an inverted index mapping words to document IDs where they appear. """
    for doc_id, content in docs.items():
        # Normalize and split words
```

```
            words = re.findall(r'\b\w+\b', content.lower())
            for word in words:
                inverted_index[word].add(doc_id)

# Building the index
build_inverted_index(documents)

# Function to perform search
def search(query):
    """ Search the inverted index for documents containing the query word. """
    return inverted_index[query.lower()]

# Example search queries
print("Documents containing 'python':", search('Python'))
print("Documents containing 'programming':", search('programming'))
print("Documents containing 'language':", search('language'))

# Output:
# Documents containing 'python': {1, 2, 4}
# Documents containing 'programming': {1, 4}
# Documents containing 'language': {1, 3}
```

Explanation

- Data Preparation: The documents are preprocessed to extract words (using regex to handle tokenization).
- Inverted Index Creation: Using a defaultdict initialized with set, each word is mapped to a set of document IDs. This structure is ideal because each word may appear in multiple documents, and sets automatically handle duplicate entries.
- Index Building: As each word is found in the documents, it's added to the inverted_index with the current document's ID. If the word isn't already in the index, defaultdict creates a new set automatically.
- Searching: The search function directly accesses the defaultdict to retrieve document IDs for any given word efficiently.

Benefits of Using defaultdict

- Automatic Handling of Missing Keys: When a new word is encountered, defaultdict automatically creates a new set for it, avoiding key errors or the need to check if the key exists.
- Simplification of Code: The code is simpler and clearer without manual checks for existence or initialization of keys.

- Efficiency: Accessing and updating the index is efficient and straightforward, making it well-suited for scenarios with large datasets and frequent queries.

Conclusion

This example demonstrates the powerful application of defaultdict in building an inverted index for a text search system, a critical component in search technologies. Using defaultdict simplifies the implementation of complex data structures and ensures efficient, error-free data handling, especially useful in fields like natural language processing and information retrieval systems.

Example 2.40
GUI Tkinter for Building an Inverted Index for Document Search

To create a feature-rich, real-time graphical user interface (GUI) using Tkinter that allows users to interact with a document corpus and perform searches using an inverted index, we will develop a Python class-based application. This GUI will enable users to visualize the distribution of words across documents and search for documents containing specific words dynamically.

Step 1: Define the GUI Class for Document Search

We'll set up the main class for our GUI, which will handle the initialization of the main window and provide methods for building an inverted index, performing searches, and displaying results.

```
import tkinter as tk
from tkinter import ttk, simpledialog, scrolledtext
from collections import defaultdict
import re

class DocumentSearchApp:
    def __init__(self, master):
        self.master = master
        self.master.title("Document Search Engine")
        self.master.geometry("600x400")

        # Initialize documents
        self.documents = {
            1: "Python is an interpreted high-level general-purpose programming language.",
```

```
            2: "Python's design philosophy emphasizes code readability with its notable
use of significant whitespace.",
            3: "Its language constructs and object-oriented approach aim to help
programmers write clear, logical code for small and large-scale projects.",
            4: "Python supports multiple programming paradigms, including structured
(particularly, procedural), object-oriented, and functional programming."
        }

        # Initialize inverted index
        self.inverted_index = defaultdict(set)
        self.build_inverted_index()

        # GUI Setup
        self.setup_widgets()

    def setup_widgets(self):
        # Text box for search input
        self.search_entry = ttk.Entry(self.master, width=50)
        self.search_entry.pack(pady=20)

        # Button to perform search
        ttk.Button(self.master, text="Search", command=self.perform_search).pack()

        # Scrolled text box to display search results
        self.results_display = scrolledtext.ScrolledText(self.master, height=10, width=75)
        self.results_display.pack(pady=20)

    def build_inverted_index(self):
        """ Build an inverted index mapping words to document IDs where they appear. """
        for doc_id, content in self.documents.items():
            words = re.findall(r'\b\w+\b', content.lower())
            for word in words:
                self.inverted_index[word].add(doc_id)

    def perform_search(self):
        """ Search the inverted index for documents containing the query word. """
        query = self.search_entry.get().lower()
        document_ids = self.inverted_index[query]
        self.display_results(query, document_ids)

    def display_results(self, query, document_ids):
        """ Display the search results in the text box. """
        self.results_display.delete('1.0', tk.END)
        if document_ids:
            results = ', '.join(str(doc_id) for doc_id in document_ids)
            self.results_display.insert(tk.END, f"Documents containing '{query}': {results}")
        else:
```

```
            self.results_display.insert(tk.END, f"No documents contain the word '{query}'.")

if __name__ == "__main__":
    root = tk.Tk()
    app = DocumentSearchApp(root)
    root.mainloop()
```

Explanation of the Code

1. Class Definition (DocumentSearchApp):
   Initializes the main window and sets up GUI components for entering search queries, performing searches, and displaying results.
2. Widget Setup (setup_widgets):
   Configures the GUI layout with an entry field for search queries, a button to trigger searches, and a scrolled text area for displaying search results.
3. Inverted Index Construction (build_inverted_index):
   Constructs an inverted index from the document corpus, mapping each unique word to the set of document IDs in which it appears.
4. Search Execution (perform_search):
   Retrieves the query from the entry field, looks up the query in the inverted index, and calls display_results to show the documents containing the queried word.
5. Results Display (display_results):
   Updates the results display area to show which documents contain the queried word or informs the user if no documents contain the word.

Features of the GUI

- Interactive Document Search: Allows users to search for words across multiple documents dynamically.
- Real-Time Search Results: Provides immediate feedback on search queries, showing where each word appears in the document corpus.
- User-Friendly Interface: Offers a clean, intuitive interface with straightforward controls for search input and results display, making it accessible for users of all skill levels.

This GUI application provides a practical tool for searching and analyzing text documents, ideal for educational purposes, preliminary data analysis, or simply exploring content dynamically.

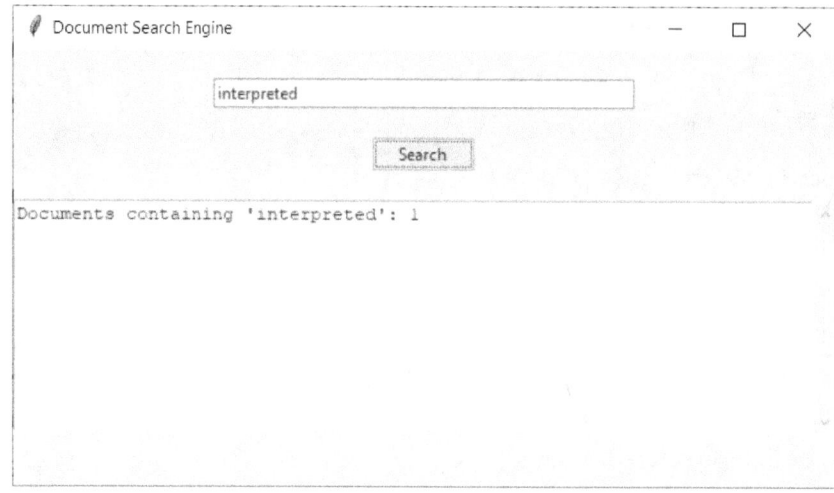

Example 2.41

Transportation Network Analysis

Dictionaries are exceptionally useful in representing graph data structures due to their flexible, intuitive, and efficient mapping of relationships between nodes. This capability makes dictionaries ideal for managing complex networked data, such as in social networks, transportation routes, or even dependency graphs in software or systems design.

Consider a real-world scenario where you need to manage and analyze a transportation network. This network comprises various stations as nodes and direct routes between them as edges. Each route may have attributes such as distance, travel time, and cost. A dictionary-based representation of this graph allows you to efficiently store and query the network data.

Scenario Setup

Imagine managing a simplified rail or bus network where stations are connected by direct routes. You want to store information about each route and be able to quickly find all routes from a given station, assess the costs, or even update the network as routes are added or removed.

Implementation Using Nested Dictionaries

Here's how you could implement and use a graph structure to represent and manipulate this transportation network:

```
# Graph using nested dictionaries
```

```python
# Outer dictionary keys are station names, values are dictionaries of
neighboring stations with edge attributes
network = {
    "StationA": {"StationB": {"distance": 5, "time": 10, "cost": 2},
                 "StationC": {"distance": 3, "time": 7, "cost": 5}},
    "StationB": {"StationA": {"distance": 5, "time": 10, "cost": 2},
                 "StationD": {"distance": 4, "time": 5, "cost": 3}},
    "StationC": {"StationA": {"distance": 3, "time": 7, "cost": 5},
                 "StationD": {"distance": 2, "time": 3, "cost": 3}},
    "StationD": {"StationB": {"distance": 4, "time": 5, "cost": 3},
                 "StationC": {"distance": 2, "time": 3, "cost": 3}}
}

def add_route(from_station, to_station, distance, time, cost):
    if from_station not in network:
        network[from_station] = {}
    network[from_station][to_station] = {"distance": distance, "time": time, "cost": cost}

def remove_route(from_station, to_station):
    if from_station in network and to_station in network[from_station]:
        del network[from_station][to_station]

def get_routes_from_station(station):
    if station in network:
        return network[station]
    else:
        return "No routes from this station."

# Example usage
add_route("StationA", "StationE", 10, 20, 7)
remove_route("StationC", "StationD")
print("Routes from StationA:", get_routes_from_station("StationA"))
print("Routes from StationC:", get_routes_from_station("StationC"))

# Output:
# Routes from StationA: {'StationB': {'distance': 5, 'time': 10, 'cost': 2}, 'StationC': {'distance': 3, 'time': 7, 'cost': 5}, 'StationE': {'distance': 10, 'time': 20, 'cost': 7}}
# Routes from StationC: {'StationA': {'distance': 3, 'time': 7, 'cost': 5}}
```

Explanation

- Network Representation: The network is represented as a dictionary of dictionaries. Each key in the outer dictionary is a station, and each value is another

dictionary representing stations reachable from this station along with the attributes of each route (distance, time, cost).
- Adding and Removing Routes: Functions add_route and remove_route allow you to dynamically update the network. This is particularly useful as transportation routes may change frequently due to construction, policy changes, or extensions of the network.
- Querying Routes: The function get_routes_from_station provides a simple way to access all routes departing from a given station, showcasing the convenience and efficiency of dictionary-based graph representations.

Conclusion

This example illustrates how dictionaries can effectively represent and manipulate graph structures in complex real-world applications such as transportation networks. Using nested dictionaries to model graphs provides a flexible, efficient, and intuitive approach to managing relational data, which is crucial for tasks involving network traversal, analysis, and real-time updates.

Example 2.42
GUI Tkinter for Transportation Network Analysis
To create an engaging and interactive real-time graphical user interface (GUI) using Tkinter for managing a transportation network graph, where stations are connected with routes that have attributes like distance, time, and cost, we'll develop a Python class-based application. This GUI will allow users to add, remove, and view routes dynamically between stations.

Step 1: Define the GUI Class for Network Management
We'll set up the main class for our GUI, which will manage the initialization of the main window and provide methods for adding, removing, and viewing routes in the network.

```
import tkinter as tk
from tkinter import ttk, simpledialog, messagebox

class NetworkManagerApp:
    def __init__(self, master):
        self.master = master
        self.master.title("Network Manager")
        self.master.geometry("600x400")
```

```python
        # Initialize the network graph
        self.network = {
            "StationA": {"StationB": {"distance": 5, "time": 10, "cost": 2},
                         "StationC": {"distance": 3, "time": 7, "cost": 5},
                         "StationE": {"distance": 10, "time": 20, "cost": 7}},
            "StationB": {"StationA": {"distance": 5, "time": 10, "cost": 2},
                         "StationD": {"distance": 4, "time": 5, "cost": 3}},
            "StationC": {"StationA": {"distance": 3, "time": 7, "cost": 5}},
            "StationD": {"StationB": {"distance": 4, "time": 5, "cost": 3},
                         "StationC": {"distance": 2, "time": 3, "cost": 3}}
        }

        # GUI Setup
        self.setup_widgets()

    def setup_widgets(self):
        # Buttons for managing routes
        ttk.Button(self.master, text="Add Route", command=self.add_route).pack(pady=10)
        ttk.Button(self.master, text="Remove Route", command=self.remove_route).pack(pady=10)
        ttk.Button(self.master, text="Show Routes", command=self.show_routes).pack(pady=10)

        # Text box to display routes
        self.text_display = tk.Text(self.master, height=20, width=70)
        self.text_display.pack(pady=20)

    def add_route(self):
        # Dialogs to get route information
        from_station = simpledialog.askstring("Add Route", "Enter starting station:")
        to_station = simpledialog.askstring("Add Route", "Enter destination station:")
        distance = simpledialog.askinteger("Add Route", "Enter distance:")
        time = simpledialog.askinteger("Add Route", "Enter travel time:")
        cost = simpledialog.askinteger("Add Route", "Enter travel cost:")

        # Adding route to the network
        if from_station not in self.network:
            self.network[from_station] = {}
        self.network[from_station][to_station] = {"distance": distance, "time": time, "cost": cost}

        messagebox.showinfo("Route Added", f"Route from {from_station} to {to_station} added.")
        self.show_routes()

    def remove_route(self):
        from_station = simpledialog.askstring("Remove Route", "Enter starting station:")
```

```
        to_station = simpledialog.askstring("Remove Route", "Enter destination
station:")
        if from_station in self.network and to_station in self.network[from_station]:
            del self.network[from_station][to_station]
            messagebox.showinfo("Route Removed", f"Route from {from_station} to
{to_station} removed.")
        else:
            messagebox.showerror("Error", "Route not found.")
        self.show_routes()

    def show_routes(self):
        self.text_display.delete('1.0', tk.END)
        for station, routes in self.network.items():
            self.text_display.insert(tk.END, f"Routes from {station}:\n")
            for dest, attrs in routes.items():
                self.text_display.insert(tk.END, f"  To {dest}: {attrs}\n")

if __name__ == "__main__":
    root = tk.Tk()
    app = NetworkManagerApp(root)
    root.mainloop()
```

Explanation of the Code

1. Class Definition (NetworkManagerApp):
   Initializes the main window and sets up GUI components for managing network routes.
2. Widget Setup (setup_widgets):
   Configures the GUI layout with buttons for adding, removing, and showing routes, along with a text box for displaying detailed information about all routes.
3. Route Management Functions (add_route, remove_route, show_routes):
   - add_route: Allows the user to input new route details and updates the network graph accordingly.
   - remove_route: Lets the user specify which route to remove from the network.
   - show_routes: Displays all the routes in the network along with their attributes in the text box.

Features of the GUI

- Dynamic Network Configuration: Users can dynamically configure the network by adding or removing routes.

- Real-Time Updates: Provides real-time feedback on network configuration changes, enhancing user interaction and understanding of network topology.
- Detailed Network Visualization: Shows detailed network configurations and updates, making it easier for users to visualize and manage complex networks.

This GUI application serves as a practical tool for managing and visualizing transportation or communication networks, ideal for educational purposes or network design simulations.

Example 2.43
Software Package Dependency Resolver
Let's consider a complex real-world example that involves using dictionaries to represent and solve problems in a dependency resolution system for package management. This type of system is commonly used in software development to handle dependencies between various software packages or modules, such as in package managers like pip for Python or npm for Node.js.

In this scenario, each software package may depend on several other packages. The goal is to ensure that dependencies for any given package are resolved in an order that respects the dependency constraints. That is, a package must be installed only after all the packages it depends on are installed.

Scenario Setup
Suppose you are building a system that needs to determine the correct order of package installations based on dependencies. A graph can be used where each node represents a package, and directed edges represent dependencies (an edge from A to B means A depends on B).

Implementation Using Dictionaries
Here's how you could implement this dependency resolution using dictionaries:

```python
from collections import deque, defaultdict

# Dictionary to store package dependencies as a graph
dependencies = {
    "packageA": ["packageB", "packageC"],
    "packageB": ["packageD"],
    "packageC": ["packageD", "packageE"],
    "packageD": [],
    "packageE": ["packageF"],
    "packageF": []
}

# Function to perform a topological sort using Kahn's Algorithm to resolve dependencies
def resolve_dependencies(packages):
    # Build the adjacency list and the in-degree counts
    in_degree = defaultdict(int)
    graph = defaultdict(list)

    for package, deps in packages.items():
        for dep in deps:
            graph[dep].append(package)
            in_degree[package] += 1

    # Queue for packages with no dependencies
    queue = deque([pkg for pkg in packages if in_degree[pkg] == 0])
    sorted_order = []

    while queue:
        pkg = queue.popleft()
        sorted_order.append(pkg)
```

```
        # Decrease the in-degree of each neighbor
        for neighbor in graph[pkg]:
            in_degree[neighbor] -= 1
            if in_degree[neighbor] == 0:
                queue.append(neighbor)

    # Check if there was a cycle in the graph
    if len(sorted_order) != len(packages):
        return "Dependency resolution error: cycle detected"
    return sorted_order

# Example usage
install_order = resolve_dependencies(dependencies)
print("Install order:", install_order)
```

Explanation

- Graph Representation: Packages and their dependencies are stored in a dictionary, where each key is a package, and the value is a list of packages it depends on.
- Topological Sorting: The algorithm used to resolve the dependencies is known as Kahn's algorithm for topological sorting. This algorithm is suited for handling directed acyclic graphs (DAGs), which is typical in dependency resolution scenarios.
- Cycle Detection: The algorithm includes a mechanism to detect cycles in the dependency graph, which would indicate an error in dependency specifications (e.g., circular dependencies).
- Order of Installation: The result is an order in which packages can be safely installed so that all dependencies for any given package are already installed when it is installed.

Conclusion

This example illustrates a sophisticated application of dictionaries in representing and solving graph-based problems, specifically in a software package dependency resolver system. Using dictionaries to model such complex data structures allows efficient access and manipulation of the nodes (packages) and edges (dependencies), crucial for achieving correct and efficient dependency resolution in software development and distribution environments.

Example 2.44
GUI Tkinter for Software Package Dependency Resolver
To create an advanced and interactive real-time graphical user interface (GUI) using Tkinter that visualizes the resolution of package dependencies through a topological sort, we'll develop a Python class-based application. This GUI will allow users to dynamically input package dependencies, perform the sorting, and view the order in which packages should be installed to respect their dependencies.

Step 1: Define the GUI Class for Dependency Resolution
We'll set up the main class for our GUI, which will manage the initialization of the main window and provide methods for adding dependencies, resolving them using Kahn's Algorithm, and displaying the sorted order or detecting cycles.

```python
import tkinter as tk
from tkinter import ttk, simpledialog, messagebox
from collections import deque, defaultdict

class DependencyResolverApp:
    def __init__(self, master):
        self.master = master
        self.master.title("Dependency Resolver")
        self.master.geometry("600x400")

        # Initialize the package dependencies dictionary
        self.dependencies = {
            "packageA": ["packageB", "packageC"],
            "packageB": ["packageD"],
            "packageC": ["packageD", "packageE"],
            "packageD": [],
            "packageE": ["packageF"],
            "packageF": []
        }

        # GUI Setup
        self.setup_widgets()

    def setup_widgets(self):
        # Button to add new dependency
        ttk.Button(self.master, text="Add Dependency", command=self.add_dependency).pack(pady=10)

        # Button to resolve dependencies
        ttk.Button(self.master, text="Resolve Dependencies", command=self.resolve_and_display).pack(pady=10)
```

```python
        # Text box to display results or errors
        self.text_display = tk.Text(self.master, height=20, width=70)
        self.text_display.pack(pady=20)

    def add_dependency(self):
        # Dialog to get new dependency information
        package = simpledialog.askstring("Package", "Enter the package name:")
        dependency = simpledialog.askstring("Dependency", "Enter the dependency name (comma-separated for multiple):")
        if package and dependency:
            self.dependencies[package] = dependency.split(',')
            messagebox.showinfo("Dependency Added", f"Added dependencies for {package}.")
        self.text_display.insert(tk.END, f"Current Dependencies: {self.dependencies}\n")

    def resolve_and_display(self):
        """ Resolve dependencies and display the sorted order or error message. """
        result = self.resolve_dependencies(self.dependencies)
        self.text_display.delete('1.0', tk.END)
        if isinstance(result, str):
            messagebox.showerror("Error", result)
        else:
            self.text_display.insert(tk.END, "Install order: " + ', '.join(result) + "\n")

    def resolve_dependencies(self, packages):
        """ Perform a topological sort using Kahn's Algorithm. """
        in_degree = defaultdict(int)
        graph = defaultdict(list)

        for package, deps in packages.items():
            for dep in deps:
                graph[dep].append(package)
                in_degree[package] += 1

        queue = deque([pkg for pkg in packages if in_degree[pkg] == 0])
        sorted_order = []

        while queue:
            pkg = queue.popleft()
            sorted_order.append(pkg)

            for neighbor in graph[pkg]:
                in_degree[neighbor] -= 1
                if in_degree[neighbor] == 0:
                    queue.append(neighbor)

        if len(sorted_order) != len(packages):
            return "Dependency resolution error: cycle detected"
```

```
        return sorted_order

if __name__ == "__main__":
    root = tk.Tk()
    app = DependencyResolverApp(root)
    root.mainloop()
```

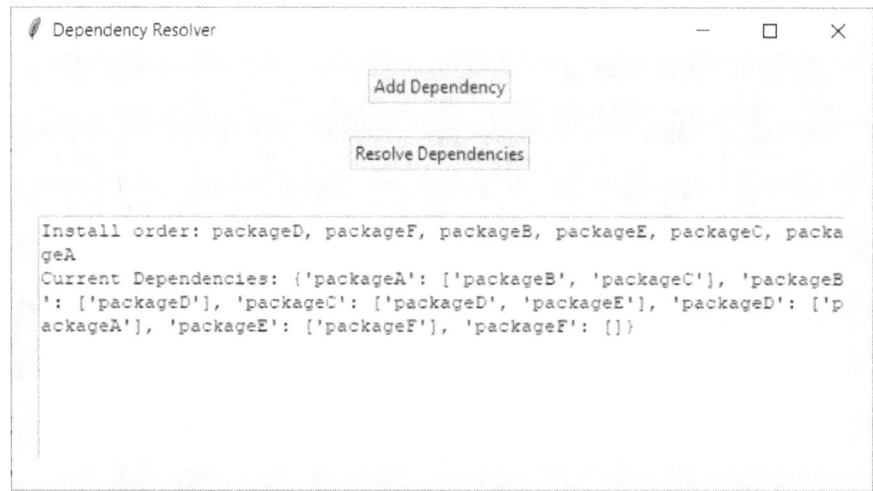

Explanation of the Code
1. Class Definition (DependencyResolverApp):
   Initializes the main window and sets up GUI components for adding package dependencies, resolving them, and displaying the results or errors.
2. Widget Setup (setup_widgets):
   Configures the GUI with buttons to add dependencies and resolve them, and a text box for displaying the installation order or errors.
3. Dependency Management (add_dependency and resolve_and_display):
   - add_dependency: Allows users to dynamically add new dependencies to the system.
   - resolve_and_display: Initiates the dependency resolution process using Kahn's Algorithm and displays the sorted order or error messages in the text box.

Features of the GUI
- Interactive Dependency Input: Users can input new package dependencies, expanding the dependency graph dynamically.

- Real-Time Dependency Resolution: Visualizes the resolution process, showing the order in which packages can be safely installed or detecting dependency cycles.
- Educational Tool: Provides a practical demonstration of Kahn's Algorithm for topological sorting, useful for educational purposes in understanding algorithms and software dependency management.

This GUI application offers a practical tool for managing and visualizing package dependencies, making it ideal for developers, educators, or anyone interested in software dependency management or algorithm visualization.

Example 2.45
Handling Configuration Data for a Distributed System

Python's interaction with JSON (JavaScript Object Notation) is crucial in modern software development, particularly for web APIs, configurations, data storage, and communication between different parts of a system or different systems entirely. JSON is a lightweight data interchange format that is easy for humans to read and write, and easy for machines to parse and generate. Python dictionaries can be seamlessly converted to JSON strings and vice versa, making them an essential tool for handling JSON data.

Imagine you are developing a distributed application where multiple services require configuration data. These configurations include information like service endpoints, database connections, authentication details, and operational parameters. To manage this efficiently, configurations are stored in JSON format and distributed to various components of the system as needed.

Scenario Setup

Suppose your application has several microservices, and each service's configuration needs to be stored, retrieved, and occasionally updated. This configuration data is shared via a central repository that other services can query to fetch their configurations.

Implementation Using Python and JSON

Here's how you might implement a simple configuration management system that stores, retrieves, and updates configurations in JSON format:

```
import json
```

```python
# Sample configuration data as a dictionary
configurations = {
    "databaseService": {
        "endpoint": "http://db.example.com",
        "port": 5432,
        "credentials": {
            "username": "admin",
            "password": "securepassword123"
        }
    },
    "authenticationService": {
        "endpoint": "http://auth.example.com",
        "port": 5000,
        "credentials": {
            "apiKey": "abcdef123456"
        }
    }
}

# Function to convert dictionary to JSON string
def save_config_to_json(config_dict):
    # Convert dictionary to JSON string
    json_str = json.dumps(config_dict, indent=4)
    # For demonstration, we'll just print the JSON. In a real system, you'd save this to a file or database.
    print(json_str)

# Function to load JSON string back into a dictionary
def load_config_from_json(json_str):
    # Convert JSON string back to dictionary
    return json.loads(json_str)

# Function to update configuration
def update_config(config_dict, service_name, key, value):
    # Navigate through nested dictionaries if necessary
    keys = key.split('.')
    last_key = keys.pop()
    sub_config = config_dict[service_name]
    for k in keys:
        sub_config = sub_config.setdefault(k, {})  # Ensure nested dictionaries exist
    sub_config[last_key] = value
    return config_dict

# Update the database port
configurations = update_config(configurations, "databaseService", "port", 5433)
```

```
# Save and load the configuration as JSON
save_config_to_json(configurations)
loaded_config = load_config_from_json(json.dumps(configurations))

# Example of how to access a nested value
print("Loaded Configuration, Database Port:", loaded_config["databaseService"]["port"])
```

Explanation
- Dictionary Representation: The configurations are initially represented as nested dictionaries, which is intuitive and easy to manipulate within Python.
- JSON Conversion: The json.dumps() function converts the Python dictionary into a JSON-formatted string, which can be saved to a file or sent over a network. Conversely, json.loads() parses a JSON string back into a Python dictionary.
- Configuration Update: The update_config function demonstrates how you can navigate and modify nested dictionaries safely, even ensuring that missing paths are created as needed (useful for dynamic updates to the configuration).

Conclusion

This example illustrates a practical use of Python dictionaries for managing configuration data in JSON format, focusing on converting between dictionaries and JSON, as well as handling nested updates. This pattern is widely applicable in software development for configuration management, data interchange between systems, and more, leveraging Python's robust JSON support to integrate smoothly with web technologies and services.

Example 2.46
GUI Tkinter for Handling Configuration Data for a Distributed System
To create a sophisticated real-time graphical user interface (GUI) using Tkinter that allows users to manage and interact with configuration data, and also supports operations such as saving to and loading from JSON format, we will develop a Python class-based application. This GUI will enable users to modify configurations dynamically, view their changes in a structured format, and understand JSON serialization and deserialization processes.

Step 1: Define the GUI Class for Configuration Management
We will set up the main class for our GUI, which will handle initializing the main window and provide methods for managing configuration data, saving it as JSON, and reloading it from JSON.

```
import tkinter as tk
from tkinter import ttk, scrolledtext, simpledialog, messagebox
import json

class ConfigManagerApp:
    def __init__(self, master):
        self.master = master
        self.master.title("Configuration Manager")
        self.master.geometry("600x400")

        # Initialize the configuration data
        self.configurations = {
            "databaseService": {
                "endpoint": "http://db.example.com",
                "port": 5432,
                "credentials": {
                    "username": "admin",
                    "password": "securepassword123"
                }
            },
            "authenticationService": {
                "endpoint": "http://auth.example.com",
                "port": 5000,
                "credentials": {
                    "apiKey": "abcdef123456"
                }
            }
        }

        # GUI Setup
        self.setup_widgets()

    def setup_widgets(self):
        # Text box to display and edit JSON
        self.text_display = scrolledtext.ScrolledText(self.master, height=20, width=75)
        self.text_display.pack(pady=10)

        # Button to save JSON to configuration
```

```python
        ttk.Button(self.master,                    text="Save           JSON",
command=self.save_json).pack(pady=10)

        # Button to load JSON from configuration
        ttk.Button(self.master,                    text="Load           JSON",
command=self.load_json).pack(pady=10)

        # Display initial configuration as JSON
        self.load_json()

    def save_json(self):
        """ Save the current JSON displayed in the text box into the
configuration dictionary. """
        json_str = self.text_display.get('1.0', tk.END)
        try:
            self.configurations = json.loads(json_str)
            messagebox.showinfo("Success", "Configuration saved successfully
from JSON.")
        except json.JSONDecodeError:
            messagebox.showerror("Error", "Invalid JSON format.")

    def load_json(self):
        """ Load the current configuration dictionary into the text box as
JSON. """
        json_str = json.dumps(self.configurations, indent=4)
        self.text_display.delete('1.0', tk.END)
        self.text_display.insert('1.0', json_str)

if __name__ == "__main__":
    root = tk.Tk()
    app = ConfigManagerApp(root)
    root.mainloop()
```

Explanation of the Code
Class Definition (ConfigManagerApp):
1. Initializes the main window and sets up GUI components for interacting with JSON configuration data.
2. Widget Setup (setup_widgets):
   Configures the GUI layout with a scrolled text box for displaying and editing JSON data, and buttons to save changes to the configuration or reload the configuration from the text box.
3. Configuration Management Functions (save_json, load_json):

- save_json: Attempts to parse JSON from the text box into the configuration dictionary, showing a success message or an error if the JSON is invalid.
- load_json: Serializes the current configuration dictionary to a JSON string and loads it into the text box for viewing and editing.

Features of the GUI
- Dynamic JSON Editing and Viewing: Users can directly edit configuration data in JSON format and see their changes reflected in real-time.
- Error Handling for JSON Operations: Provides error messages for incorrect JSON formats, helping users to correct their inputs.
- Flexibility and Real-time Feedback: Offers an intuitive interface for managing complex configurations, suitable for developers or administrators managing application settings or learning about JSON.

This GUI application serves as an effective tool for managing and visualizing JSON-based configurations, ideal for educational purposes, development environments, or any scenario where configuration data needs to be frequently accessed and modified.

```
{
    "databaseService": {
        "endpoint": "http://db.example.com",
        "port": 5432,
        "credentials": {
            "username": "admin",
            "password": "securepassword123"
        }
    },
    "authenticationService": {
        "endpoint": "http://auth.example.com",
        "port": 5000,
        "credentials": {
            "apiKey": "abcdef123456"
        }
    }
}
```

Example 2.47
E-commerce Transaction Analytics
Let's explore a more complex real-world example that involves JSON interaction with Python dictionaries in the context of data aggregation and transformation for an analytics dashboard. In this scenario, we will simulate the process of collecting, transforming, and summarizing data from multiple sources, such as user activities or transactions, and then presenting this data as JSON for consumption by a web-based analytics dashboard.

Suppose you are tasked with developing a backend system for an e-commerce platform's analytics dashboard. This dashboard needs to aggregate data about user purchases, categorize them by product categories, and calculate total sales, average sales, and number of transactions per category. The data is collected in real-time, stored in JSON format, and needs to be dynamically processed and served to the frontend.

Setup and Implementation Using Python and JSON
Here's how you might implement this system using Python dictionaries and JSON interaction:

```
import json
from collections import defaultdict

# Simulated incoming transaction data (normally this would come from a database or external API)
transactions = [
    {"id": 1, "user": "Alice", "category": "Electronics", "amount": 250.00},
    {"id": 2, "user": "Bob", "category": "Books", "amount": 23.50},
    {"id": 3, "user": "Alice", "category": "Electronics", "amount": 499.99},
    {"id": 4, "user": "Dave", "category": "Clothes", "amount": 59.90},
    {"id": 5, "user": "Alice", "category": "Books", "amount": 15.00},
    {"id": 6, "user": "Carol", "category": "Electronics", "amount": 299.95},
    {"id": 7, "user": "Carol", "category": "Books", "amount": 12.95},
    {"id": 8, "user": "Eve", "category": "Electronics", "amount": 89.95},
    {"id": 9, "user": "Alice", "category": "Books", "amount": 8.99}
]

# Aggregate data by category
category_stats = defaultdict(lambda: {"total_sales": 0, "transactions": 0, "average": 0})
for transaction in transactions:
    category = transaction["category"]
    amount = transaction["amount"]
    category_stats[category]["total_sales"] += amount
    category_stats[category]["transactions"] += 1
```

```
# Calculate average sales per category
for category, stats in category_stats.items():
    stats["average"] = stats["total_sales"] / stats["transactions"]

# Convert aggregated data to JSON for transmission to a web frontend
json_output = json.dumps(category_stats, indent=4)
print(json_output)

# Example Output:
"""
{
    "Electronics": {
        "total_sales": 1139.89,
        "transactions": 4,
        "average": 284.9725
    },
    "Books": {
        "total_sales": 60.44,
        "transactions": 4,
        "average": 15.11
    },
    "Clothes": {
        "total_sales": 59.9,
        "transactions": 1,
        "average": 59.9
    }
}
"""
```

Explanation

- Data Aggregation: Transactions are processed to aggregate financial data by product category using a defaultdict. This approach simplifies accumulation without needing to check if the key already exists.
- Average Calculation: Once aggregation is complete, the average transaction value for each category is calculated.
- JSON Conversion: The aggregated and calculated data is converted into JSON format. This JSON can be easily consumed by web applications, allowing for dynamic updates and rendering on an analytics dashboard.
- Dynamic Interaction: The system handles real-time data dynamically, providing up-to-date analytics to users. Python's JSON handling capabilities facilitate easy integration with web technologies.

Conclusion

This example demonstrates the effective use of Python dictionaries for complex data manipulation tasks involving JSON data interaction—key in developing backend systems for analytics and other data-driven web applications. The scenario shows how data can be aggregated, processed, and serialized into JSON, which is a common requirement in modern web development and data analysis pipelines.

Example 2.48
GUI Tkinter E-commerce Transaction Analytics

To create a sophisticated real-time graphical user interface (GUI) using Tkinter that visualizes transaction data aggregated by category and performs computations to display totals, transactions count, and averages, I'll explain how to build a Python class-based application. This GUI will enable users to dynamically interact with the simulated transaction data, view computed statistics in various forms, and export these as JSON.

Step 1: Define the GUI Class for Transaction Data Analysis

We will set up the main class for our GUI, which will manage the initialization of the main window and provide methods for loading transaction data, performing calculations, and displaying the results visually.

```python
import tkinter as tk
from tkinter import ttk, scrolledtext
import json
from collections import defaultdict

class TransactionAnalyzerApp:
    def __init__(self, master):
        self.master = master
        self.master.title("Transaction Analyzer")
        self.master.geometry("600x400")

        # Initialize transaction data
        self.transactions = [
            {"id": 1, "user": "Alice", "category": "Electronics", "amount": 250.00},
            {"id": 2, "user": "Bob", "category": "Books", "amount": 23.50},
            {"id": 3, "user": "Alice", "category": "Electronics", "amount": 499.99},
            {"id": 4, "user": "Dave", "category": "Clothes", "amount": 59.90},
            {"id": 5, "user": "Alice", "category": "Books", "amount": 15.00},
            {"id": 6, "user": "Carol", "category": "Electronics", "amount": 299.95},
            {"id": 7, "user": "Carol", "category": "Books", "amount": 12.95},
            {"id": 8, "user": "Eve", "category": "Electronics", "amount": 89.95},
```

```python
            {"id": 9, "user": "Alice", "category": "Books", "amount": 8.99}
        ]

        # GUI Setup
        self.setup_widgets()
        self.category_stats = defaultdict(lambda: {"total_sales": 0, "transactions": 0, "average": 0})

    def setup_widgets(self):
        # Button to calculate stats
        ttk.Button(self.master, text="Calculate Stats", command=self.calculate_stats).pack(pady=10)

        # Text box to display stats
        self.stats_display = scrolledtext.ScrolledText(self.master, height=15, width=70)
        self.stats_display.pack(pady=20)

    def calculate_stats(self):
        """ Aggregate and compute stats from transactions. """
        for transaction in self.transactions:
            category = transaction["category"]
            amount = transaction["amount"]
            self.category_stats[category]["total_sales"] += amount
            self.category_stats[category]["transactions"] += 1

        for category, stats in self.category_stats.items():
            stats["average"] = stats["total_sales"] / stats["transactions"]

        self.display_stats()

    def display_stats(self):
        """ Display the computed stats in the text box. """
        json_output = json.dumps(self.category_stats, indent=4)
        self.stats_display.delete('1.0', tk.END)
        self.stats_display.insert(tk.END, json_output)

if __name__ == "__main__":
    root = tk.Tk()
    app = TransactionAnalyzerApp(root)
    root.mainloop()
```

Explanation of the Code

1. Class Definition (TransactionAnalyzerApp):
   Initializes the main window and sets up GUI components for analyzing transaction data and displaying results.
2. Widget Setup (setup_widgets):

Configures the GUI layout with a button to initiate data aggregation and a scrolled text box for displaying results.

3. Data Aggregation and Display (calculate_stats, display_stats):
   - calculate_stats: Aggregates data from transactions, calculates totals, transaction counts, and averages for each category.
   - display_stats: Serializes the computed statistics into JSON format and displays them in the text box.

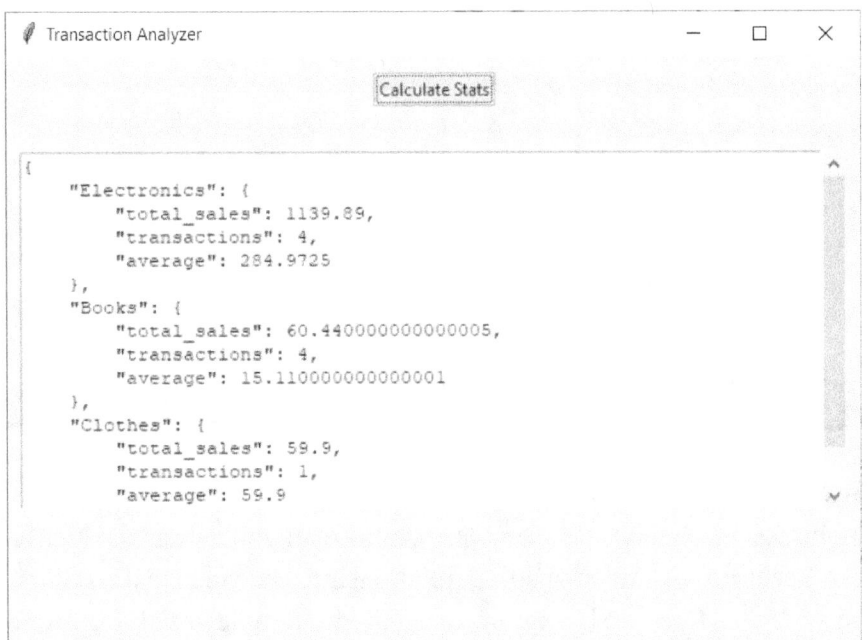

Features of the GUI
- Dynamic Data Interaction: Users can compute statistics from transaction data dynamically with the click of a button.
- Real-Time Data Visualization: Provides real-time feedback by displaying aggregated data and computed averages in a clear, readable JSON format.
- User-Friendly Interface: Offers a straightforward interface with intuitive controls for managing transaction data and viewing results, making it accessible for users of varying technical levels.

This GUI application serves as an effective tool for managing and visualizing transaction data, making it ideal for financial analysis, educational purposes, or business analytics where quick data insights are crucial.

SCIENTIFIC APPLICATIONS

SCIENTIFIC APPLICATIONS

Example 3.1

Pairwise Sequence Alignment

Using dictionaries in Python for complex scientific applications is highly effective, especially in scenarios where managing relationships between data points and rapid lookups are crucial. Here, we'll explore a detailed example involving bioinformatics, specifically the construction and use of a genetic sequence alignment tool that uses dictionaries to map genetic sequences to their corresponding identifiers and properties.

Scenario: Genetic Sequence Alignment Tool

In bioinformatics, sequence alignment is used to identify regions of similarity that may indicate functional, structural, or evolutionary relationships between the sequences. Efficiently managing and comparing these sequences is crucial for genetic research, such as identifying new genes, studying evolutionary relationships, and developing drugs.

In this example, we'll simulate the process of aligning DNA sequences using a simplified version of the Needleman-Wunsch algorithm, a classical method for global sequence alignment. We'll use dictionaries to store the sequences and scoring matrices, which are essential components of the algorithm.

Implementation Using Python Dictionaries

```python
import numpy as np

# Dictionary to hold the genetic sequences
sequences = {
    'seq1': 'GATTACA',
    'seq2': 'GCATGCU'
}

# Scoring matrix in a dictionary format: keys are tuples of (nucleotide1, nucleotide2)
match_score = 1
mismatch_penalty = -1
gap_penalty = -1

scoring_matrix = {
    ('A', 'A'): match_score,
    ('C', 'C'): match_score,
    ('G', 'G'): match_score,
    ('T', 'T'): match_score,
    ('A', 'C'): mismatch_penalty,
    ('A', 'G'): mismatch_penalty,
    ('A', 'T'): mismatch_penalty,
    ('C', 'A'): mismatch_penalty,
    ('C', 'G'): mismatch_penalty,
    ('C', 'T'): mismatch_penalty,
    ('G', 'A'): mismatch_penalty,
    ('G', 'C'): mismatch_penalty,
    ('G', 'T'): mismatch_penalty,
    ('T', 'A'): mismatch_penalty,
    ('T', 'C'): mismatch_penalty,
    ('T', 'G'): mismatch_penalty
}

def needleman_wunsch(seq1, seq2, scoring, gap_penalty):
    n, m = len(seq1), len(seq2)
    score_matrix = np.zeros((n + 1, m + 1))

    # Initialize scoring matrix and traceback path matrix
    for i in range(n + 1):
        score_matrix[i][0] = gap_penalty * i
    for j in range(m + 1):
        score_matrix[0][j] = gap_penalty * j

    # Fill in the scoring matrix
    for i in range(1, n + 1):
        for j in range(1, m + 1):
            match = score_matrix[i - 1][j - 1] + scoring.get((seq1[i - 1], seq2[j - 1]), gap_penalty)
```

```
            delete = score_matrix[i - 1][j] + gap_penalty
            insert = score_matrix[i][j - 1] + gap_penalty
            score_matrix[i][j] = max(match, delete, insert)

    return score_matrix

# Compute the alignment score matrix
alignment_score    =    needleman_wunsch(sequences['seq1'],    sequences['seq2'],
scoring_matrix, gap_penalty)

print("Alignment Score Matrix:")
print(alignment_score)
```

Explanation

- Sequence Storage: DNA sequences are stored in a dictionary with identifiers as keys, allowing for easy expansion and management of multiple sequences.
- Scoring System: Another dictionary stores the scores for matching and mismatching nucleotides, crucial for the alignment algorithm's scoring phase.
- Alignment Algorithm: The Needleman-Wunsch algorithm is implemented, utilizing the dictionaries for scoring and sequences. The score for aligning any two nucleotides is retrieved from the scoring_matrix, enabling rapid calculation and flexible adjustment of scoring parameters.
- Matrix Calculation: A matrix is used to compute alignment scores based on the dictionary-driven scoring system, facilitating efficient backtracking to determine the optimal alignment.

Conclusion

This example illustrates how dictionaries in Python can be applied to handle complex scientific tasks such as genetic sequence alignment. Dictionaries provide a robust and flexible way to manage biological data and parameter settings, allowing for efficient data retrieval and manipulation, essential for high-performance scientific computing in bioinformatics and related fields.

Example 3.2
GUI Tkinter for Pairwise Sequence Alignment

To create an advanced and interactive real-time graphical user interface (GUI) using Tkinter for visualizing the sequence alignment process through the Needleman-Wunsch algorithm, I'll describe how to build a Python class-based application. This GUI will enable users to input genetic sequences, compute the alignment using custom scoring matrices, and visually display the resulting score matrix and alignment paths.

Step 1: Define the GUI Class for Sequence Alignment

We'll set up the main class for our GUI, which will manage the initialization of the main window and provide methods for entering genetic sequences, setting scoring parameters, performing the Needleman-Wunsch algorithm, and displaying results.

```python
import tkinter as tk
from tkinter import ttk, simpledialog, messagebox
import numpy as np

class SequenceAlignmentApp:
    def __init__(self, master):
        self.master = master
        self.master.title("Sequence Alignment using Needleman-Wunsch")
        self.master.geometry("700x500")

        # Initialize scoring parameters
        self.match_score = 1
        self.mismatch_penalty = -1
        self.gap_penalty = -1
        self.sequences = {'seq1': '', 'seq2': ''}
        self.scoring_matrix = {
            ('A', 'A'): self.match_score,
            ('C', 'C'): self.match_score,
            ('G', 'G'): self.match_score,
            ('T', 'T'): self.match_score,
            ('A', 'C'): self.mismatch_penalty,
            ('A', 'G'): self.mismatch_penalty,
            ('A', 'T'): self.mismatch_penalty,
            ('C', 'A'): self.mismatch_penalty,
            ('C', 'G'): self.mismatch_penalty,
            ('C', 'T'): self.mismatch_penalty,
            ('G', 'A'): self.mismatch_penalty,
            ('G', 'C'): self.mismatch_penalty,
            ('G', 'T'): self.mismatch_penalty,
            ('T', 'A'): self.mismatch_penalty,
            ('T', 'C'): self.mismatch_penalty,
            ('T', 'G'): self.mismatch_penalty
        }

        # GUI Setup
        self.setup_widgets()

    def setup_widgets(self):
        # Entry fields for sequences
```

```python
        ttk.Label(self.master, text="Sequence 1:").pack()
        self.seq1_entry = ttk.Entry(self.master, width=50)
        self.seq1_entry.pack()

        ttk.Label(self.master, text="Sequence 2:").pack()
        self.seq2_entry = ttk.Entry(self.master, width=50)
        self.seq2_entry.pack()

        # Button to perform alignment
        ttk.Button(self.master, text="Align Sequences", command=self.perform_alignment).pack(pady=10)

        # Text box to display score matrix
        self.score_matrix_display = tk.Text(self.master, height=20, width=80)
        self.score_matrix_display.pack(pady=20)

    def perform_alignment(self):
        """ Perform the Needleman-Wunsch algorithm and display results. """
        seq1 = self.seq1_entry.get().strip().upper()
        seq2 = self.seq2_entry.get().strip().upper()
        if seq1 and seq2:
            score_matrix = self.needleman_wunsch(seq1, seq2, self.scoring_matrix, self.gap_penalty)
            self.display_score_matrix(score_matrix)
        else:
            messagebox.showerror("Error", "Please enter both sequences.")

    def needleman_wunsch(self, seq1, seq2, scoring, gap_penalty):
        """ Needleman-Wunsch algorithm to compute score matrix. """
        n, m = len(seq1), len(seq2)
        score_matrix = np.zeros((n + 1, m + 1))

        for i in range(n + 1):
            score_matrix[i][0] = gap_penalty * i
        for j in range(m + 1):
            score_matrix[0][j] = gap_penalty * j

        for i in range(1, n + 1):
            for j in range(1, m + 1):
                match = score_matrix[i - 1][j - 1] + scoring.get((seq1[i - 1], seq2[j - 1]), gap_penalty)
                delete = score_matrix[i - 1][j] + gap_penalty
                insert = score_matrix[i][j - 1] + gap_penalty
                score_matrix[i][j] = max(match, delete, insert)

        return score_matrix

    def display_score_matrix(self, score_matrix):
        """ Display the score matrix in the text box. """
        self.score_matrix_display.delete('1.0', tk.END)
```

```
            for row in score_matrix:
                self.score_matrix_display.insert(tk.END, ' '.join(f"{val:5.1f}" for val in row) + "\n")

if __name__ == "__main__":
    root = tk.Tk()
    app = SequenceAlignmentApp(root)
    root.mainloop()
```

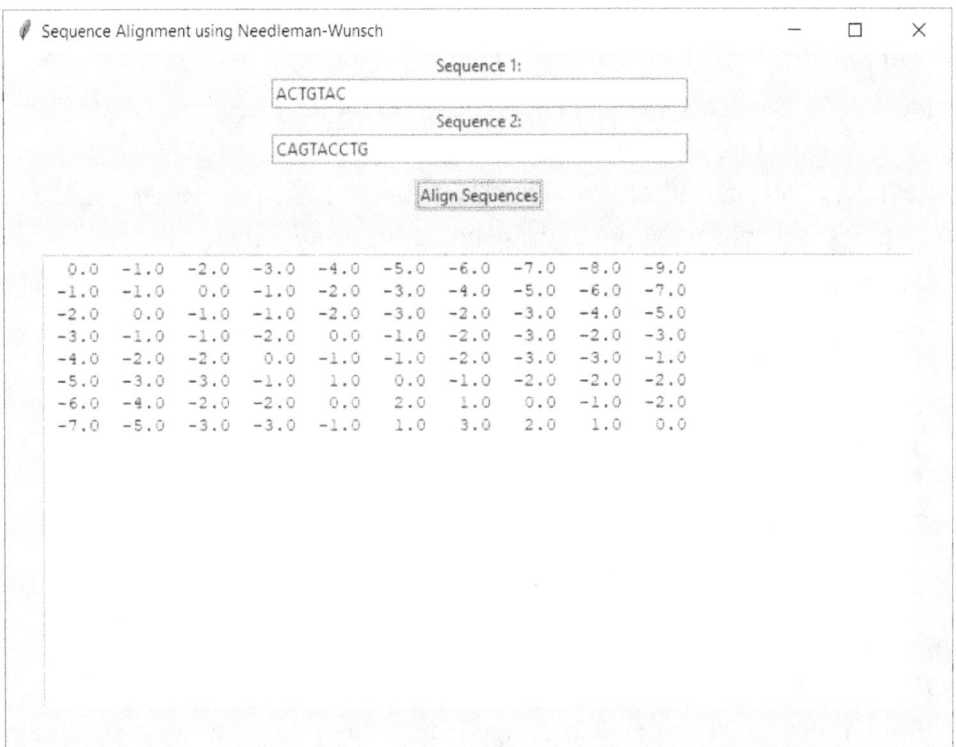

Explanation of the Code

1. Class Definition (SequenceAlignmentApp):
   Initializes the main window and sets up GUI components for sequence input, alignment computation, and displaying the score matrix.
2. Widget Setup (setup_widgets):
   Configures the GUI layout with entry fields for two sequences, a button to trigger the alignment process, and a text box to display the resulting score matrix.
3. Sequence Alignment Execution (perform_alignment, needleman_wunsch):
   - perform_alignment: Retrieves sequences from entry fields, checks if they are valid, and calls needleman_wunsch to compute the alignment.

- needleman_wunsch: Implements the Needleman-Wunsch algorithm to calculate the score matrix based on the input sequences and scoring parameters.
4. Results Display (display_score_matrix):
Formats and displays the computed score matrix in a text box, allowing users to visually inspect the alignment scores for each sequence pair.

Features of the GUI
- Interactive Sequence Alignment: Allows users to enter genetic sequences and dynamically compute their alignment.
- Real-Time Visualization: Provides immediate visual feedback by displaying the score matrix, enhancing the understanding of the alignment process.
- Customizable Scoring Parameters: Offers flexibility to adjust match scores, mismatch penalties, and gap penalties, making the tool adaptable for different sequence analysis scenarios.

This GUI application serves as an effective educational and practical tool for understanding and applying sequence alignment algorithms, particularly useful in bioinformatics and genetic research.

Example 3.3
Air Quality Analysis and Visualization

Let's explore a more complex scientific application involving the use of dictionaries in Python combined with Matplotlib for visualization. This example will focus on an environmental science application: analyzing and visualizing air quality data across different locations. Dictionaries will be used to manage the data efficiently, and Matplotlib will be employed to visualize the results in a meaningful way.

Scenario

Suppose you are working with air quality index (AQI) data collected from various monitoring stations across a large metropolitan area. The data includes readings of different pollutants like PM2.5, PM10, NO2, and O3, which are key indicators of air quality. You need to process this data, compute the average AQI for each location, and then visualize the average AQI for all locations on a single plot.

Data Setup

Here's a simplified setup with sample AQI data for different pollutants across three monitoring stations:

```
import matplotlib.pyplot as plt
import numpy as np

# Sample data: each key is a station, and each value is another dictionary of pollutant readings
air_quality_data = {
    "Station1": {"PM2.5": [55, 30, 45], "PM10": [60, 65, 70], "NO2": [25, 20, 30], "O3": [10, 12, 13]},
    "Station2": {"PM2.5": [65, 70, 75], "PM10": [80, 85, 78], "NO2": [35, 40, 45], "O3": [20, 21, 19]},
    "Station3": {"PM2.5": [40, 42, 43], "PM10": [50, 55, 53], "NO2": [20, 25, 27], "O3": [15, 17, 18]}
}

# Compute the average AQI for each station
avg_aqi = {}
for station, pollutants in air_quality_data.items():
    total_aqi = 0
    count = 0
    for readings in pollutants.values():
        total_aqi += np.mean(readings)
        count += 1
    avg_aqi[station] = total_aqi / count

# Plotting the average AQI using Matplotlib
stations = list(avg_aqi.keys())
aqi_values = list(avg_aqi.values())

plt.figure(figsize=(10, 5))
plt.bar(stations, aqi_values, color='blue')
plt.xlabel('Station')
plt.ylabel('Average AQI')
plt.title('Average Air Quality Index (AQI) by Station')
plt.ylim(0, max(aqi_values) + 10)  # Set y-axis limits to make the chart clearer
plt.show()
```

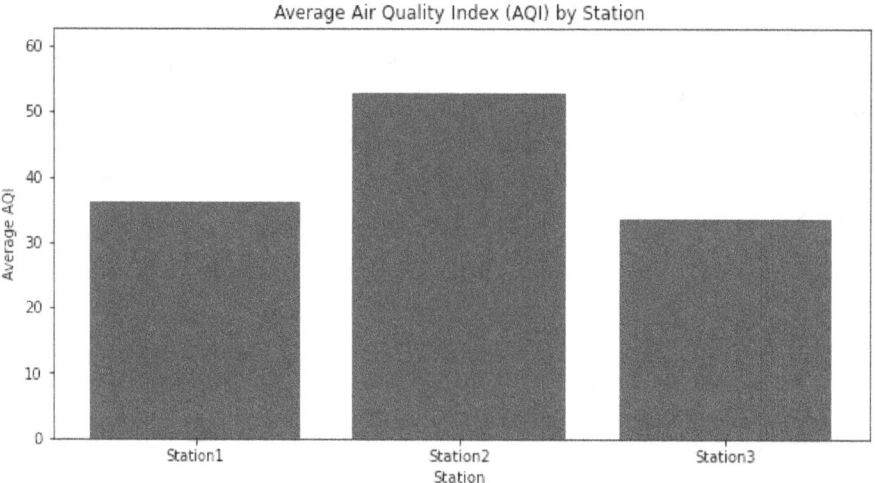

Explanation

- Data Organization: Air quality readings are stored in a nested dictionary where each key is a monitoring station and the value is another dictionary containing lists of pollutant measurements.
- Data Processing: The average AQI for each station is computed by averaging the means of each pollutant's readings. This involves iterating over the dictionary, accessing each list of pollutant data, calculating the mean, and then averaging these means.
- Visualization: The computed average AQIs are then visualized using a bar chart in Matplotlib. Each station is represented on the x-axis, and the average AQI value is represented on the y-axis.

Conclusion

This example demonstrates how dictionaries can be effectively used to handle and organize complex scientific data, facilitating easy access and manipulation. Additionally, integrating Matplotlib allows for the visualization of this data in a clear and impactful way, providing insights into air quality trends across different monitoring stations. Such applications are crucial in environmental science, where data-driven decisions and policies are needed to address air pollution and its effects on public health.

Example 3.4
GUI Tkinter for Air Quality Analysis and Visualization
To create an advanced and interactive real-time graphical user interface (GUI) using Tkinter and Matplotlib for visualizing air quality data across different stations, I'll guide you through building a Python class-based application. This GUI will enable users to interact with air quality data, compute average Air Quality Index (AQI) values, and dynamically generate bar charts to visually compare these averages across different stations.

Step 1: Define the GUI Class for Air Quality Visualization
We will set up the main class for our GUI, which will manage the initialization of the main window and provide methods for displaying air quality data and visualizing it through charts.

```
import tkinter as tk
from tkinter import ttk
import matplotlib.pyplot as plt
from matplotlib.backends.backend_tkagg import FigureCanvasTkAgg
import numpy as np

class AirQualityApp:
    def __init__(self, master):
        self.master = master
        self.master.title("Air Quality Data Visualization")
        self.master.geometry("800x600")

        # Initialize air quality data
        self.air_quality_data = {
            "Station1": {"PM2.5": [55, 30, 45], "PM10": [60, 65, 70], "NO2": [25, 20, 30], "O3": [10, 12, 13]},
            "Station2": {"PM2.5": [65, 70, 75], "PM10": [80, 85, 78], "NO2": [35, 40, 45], "O3": [20, 21, 19]},
            "Station3": {"PM2.5": [40, 42, 43], "PM10": [50, 55, 53], "NO2": [20, 25, 27], "O3": [15, 17, 18]}
        }

        # GUI Setup
        self.setup_widgets()

    def setup_widgets(self):
        # Button to compute and display AQI chart
        ttk.Button(self.master,           text="Show         AQI         Chart", command=self.plot_aqi).pack(pady=10)

        # Placeholder for the Matplotlib figure
```

```python
        self.fig, self.ax = plt.subplots(figsize=(10, 5))
        self.canvas = FigureCanvasTkAgg(self.fig, self.master)
        self.canvas.get_tk_widget().pack(fill=tk.BOTH, expand=True)

    def compute_avg_aqi(self):
        """ Compute the average AQI for each station """
        avg_aqi = {}
        for station, pollutants in self.air_quality_data.items():
            total_aqi = 0
            count = 0
            for readings in pollutants.values():
                total_aqi += np.mean(readings)
                count += 1
            avg_aqi[station] = total_aqi / count
        return avg_aqi

    def plot_aqi(self):
        """ Plot the average AQI using Matplotlib in the Tkinter window """
        avg_aqi = self.compute_avg_aqi()
        stations = list(avg_aqi.keys())
        aqi_values = list(avg_aqi.values())

        self.ax.clear()  # Clear the previous chart
        self.ax.bar(stations, aqi_values, color='blue')
        self.ax.set_xlabel('Station')
        self.ax.set_ylabel('Average AQI')
        self.ax.set_title('Average Air Quality Index (AQI) by Station')
        self.ax.set_ylim(0, max(aqi_values) + 10)  # Set y-axis limits to make the chart clearer
        self.canvas.draw()

if __name__ == "__main__":
    root = tk.Tk()
    app = AirQualityApp(root)
    root.mainloop()
```

Explanation of the Code

1. Class Definition (AirQualityApp):
   Initializes the main window and sets up GUI components for displaying AQI charts.
2. Widget Setup (setup_widgets):
   Configures the GUI layout with a button to trigger the AQI computation and chart plotting, and integrates a Matplotlib figure canvas to display the chart within the Tkinter window.
3. Data Analysis and Visualization (compute_avg_aqi, plot_aqi):

- compute_avg_aqi: Calculates the average AQI for each station based on the data.
- plot_aqi: Generates a bar chart showing the average AQI for each station, updating the chart dynamically whenever the data is recalculated or the button is pressed.

Features of the GUI

- Interactive Data Visualization: Users can interactively visualize AQI data through dynamically generated charts, providing a clear comparison between different stations.
- Integration of Matplotlib with Tkinter: Seamlessly integrates Matplotlib plots into the Tkinter application, allowing for advanced data visualization within the GUI.
- Real-Time Feedback: The application provides immediate visual updates upon user interaction, enhancing the usability and responsiveness of the GUI.

This GUI application serves as a powerful tool for environmental scientists, data analysts, or anyone interested in air quality monitoring, offering advanced visualization and data interaction capabilities.

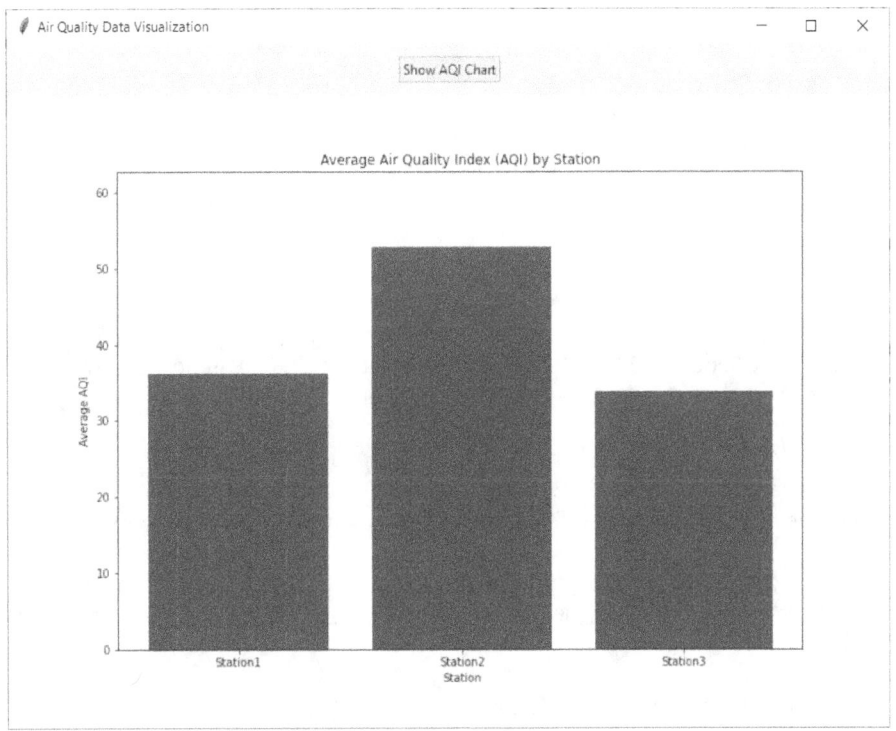

Example 3.5
Gene Expression Analysis Across Different Conditions

For a more complex scientific application involving dictionaries and visualization, let's consider a scenario in computational biology, specifically Gene Expression Heatmaps from high-throughput RNA sequencing data. This type of data visualization is critical for understanding gene expression patterns across different conditions or time points, which can inform hypotheses about genetic regulation, disease mechanisms, or treatment effects.

Imagine you are analyzing gene expression data collected under various experimental conditions (e.g., different drug treatments or environmental changes) to identify how genes respond to each condition. Each gene's expression level is measured under each condition, and you need to visualize this data to quickly discern patterns or anomalies.

Data Setup
We'll simulate a dataset where each gene's expression levels under various conditions are stored in dictionaries, and then visualize these in a heatmap using Matplotlib and Seaborn (a Python data visualization library that provides a high-level interface for drawing attractive statistical graphics).

Implementation

```
import numpy as np
import matplotlib.pyplot as plt
import seaborn as sns

# Sample data: each key is a condition, and each value is another dictionary with gene expression levels
gene_expression_data = {
    "Condition1": {"Gene1": 10, "Gene2": 200, "Gene3": 50, "Gene4": 400},
    "Condition2": {"Gene1": 20, "Gene2": 180, "Gene3": 60, "Gene4": 420},
    "Condition3": {"Gene1": 30, "Gene2": 160, "Gene3": 70, "Gene4": 440},
    "Condition4": {"Gene1": 40, "Gene2": 150, "Gene3": 80, "Gene4": 460}
}

# Convert dictionary data into a 2D NumPy array for visualization
genes = list(gene_expression_data["Condition1"].keys())  # assuming all conditions have the same genes
conditions = list(gene_expression_data.keys())
expression_matrix = np.array([[gene_expression_data[cond][gene] for gene in genes] for cond in conditions])

# Plotting the heatmap using Matplotlib and Seaborn
```

```
plt.figure(figsize=(10, 8))
sns.heatmap(expression_matrix,      annot=True,      fmt="d",      xticklabels=genes,
yticklabels=conditions, cmap="viridis")
plt.title("Gene Expression Levels Under Different Conditions")
plt.xlabel("Genes")
plt.ylabel("Conditions")
plt.show()
```

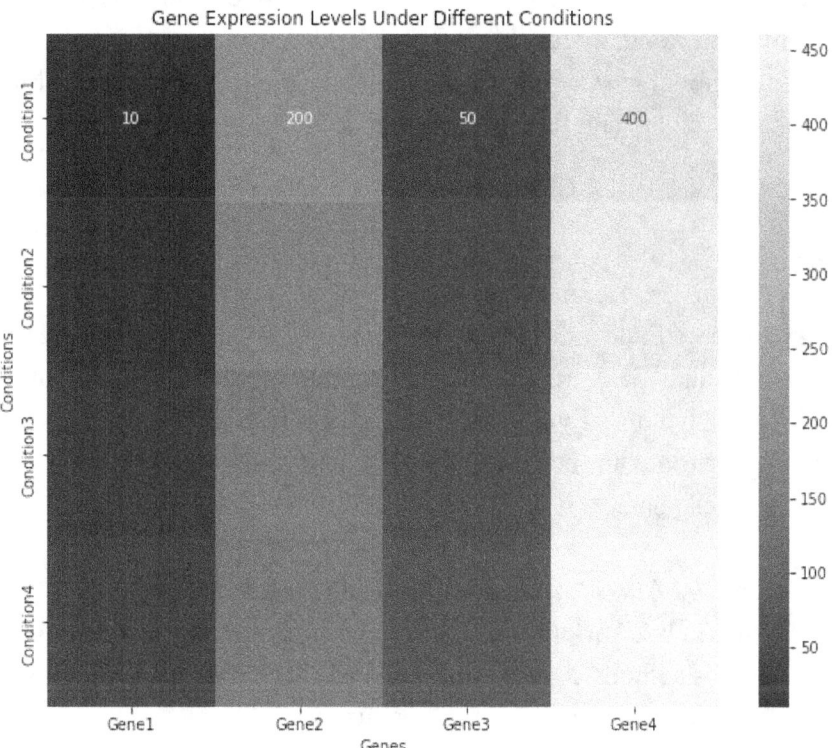

Explanation

- Data Organization: Gene expression data is structured in a nested dictionary where each key is an experimental condition and each value is another dictionary mapping genes to their expression levels under that condition.
- Data Transformation: The nested dictionary structure is transformed into a 2D NumPy array, which is suitable for heatmap visualization. This transformation requires consistent ordering of genes and conditions, which is achieved by listing the dictionary keys.
- Heatmap Visualization: The heatmap is created using Seaborn's heatmap function, which takes the 2D array of gene expression data. Genes are labeled along the x-

axis and conditions along the y-axis. The color intensity in the heatmap reflects the magnitude of gene expression.

Conclusion

This example illustrates a complex application of dictionaries for managing structured biological data and the integration of Python's powerful visualization libraries to interpret this data effectively. Heatmaps provide a comprehensive overview of the expression landscape, facilitating rapid assessment of gene behavior under various conditions. Such analyses are foundational in genomics and molecular biology research, helping scientists uncover functional insights and therapeutic targets.

Example 3.6
GUI Tkinter for Gene Expression Analysis Across Different Conditions

To build a sophisticated and interactive real-time graphical user interface (GUI) using Tkinter, Matplotlib, and Seaborn for visualizing gene expression data across different conditions, we will develop a Python class-based application. This GUI will allow users to input gene expression data, perform analyses, and dynamically generate heatmaps to visually represent these data.

Step 1: Define the GUI Class for Gene Expression Visualization

We'll set up the main class for our GUI, which will handle the initialization of the main window and provide methods for entering gene expression data, calculating expression matrices, and visualizing these matrices as heatmaps.

```
import tkinter as tk
from tkinter import ttk
import numpy as np
import matplotlib.pyplot as plt
from matplotlib.backends.backend_tkagg import FigureCanvasTkAgg
import seaborn as sns

class GeneExpressionApp:
    def __init__(self, master):
        self.master = master
        self.master.title("Gene Expression Heatmap Visualizer")
        self.master.geometry("800x600")

        # Sample gene expression data, structured for easy updating and visualization
        self.gene_expression_data = {
            "Condition1": {"Gene1": 10, "Gene2": 200, "Gene3": 50, "Gene4": 400},
```

```python
            "Condition2": {"Gene1": 20, "Gene2": 180, "Gene3": 60, "Gene4": 420},
            "Condition3": {"Gene1": 30, "Gene2": 160, "Gene3": 70, "Gene4": 440},
            "Condition4": {"Gene1": 40, "Gene2": 150, "Gene3": 80, "Gene4": 460}
        }

        # Initialize Matplotlib Figure and Seaborn style
        plt.style.use('seaborn-darkgrid')
        self.fig, self.ax = plt.subplots(figsize=(10, 8))

        # GUI Setup
        self.setup_widgets()

    def setup_widgets(self):
        # Button to refresh and redraw the heatmap
        ttk.Button(self.master, text="Draw Heatmap", command=self.draw_heatmap).pack(pady=20)

        # Canvas for Matplotlib figure
        self.canvas = FigureCanvasTkAgg(self.fig, master=self.master)
        self.canvas_widget = self.canvas.get_tk_widget()
        self.canvas_widget.pack(fill=tk.BOTH, expand=True)

    def draw_heatmap(self):
        """Generate heatmap from the current gene expression data."""
        # Prepare data
        genes = list(self.gene_expression_data["Condition1"].keys())  # Assume all conditions have the same genes
        conditions = list(self.gene_expression_data.keys())
        expression_matrix = np.array([[self.gene_expression_data[cond][gene] for gene in genes] for cond in conditions])

        # Clear the previous figure
        self.ax.clear()

        # Create heatmap using Seaborn
        sns.heatmap(expression_matrix, annot=True, fmt="d", xticklabels=genes, yticklabels=conditions, cmap="viridis", ax=self.ax)
        self.ax.set_title("Gene Expression Levels Under Different Conditions")
        self.ax.set_xlabel("Genes")
        self.ax.set_ylabel("Conditions")

        # Draw canvas
        self.canvas.draw()

if __name__ == "__main__":
    root = tk.Tk()
    app = GeneExpressionApp(root)
    root.mainloop()
```

Explanation of the Code

1. Class Definition (GeneExpressionApp):
   Initializes the main window and sets up GUI components for entering and visualizing gene expression data.
2. Widget Setup (setup_widgets):
   Configures the GUI with a button to trigger the heatmap visualization and integrates a Matplotlib figure canvas to display the heatmap within the Tkinter window.
3. Data Visualization (draw_heatmap):
   Retrieves gene expression data, converts it into a 2D NumPy array, and generates a heatmap using Seaborn. The heatmap is dynamically updated and displayed in the Tkinter window whenever the user presses the "Draw Heatmap" button.

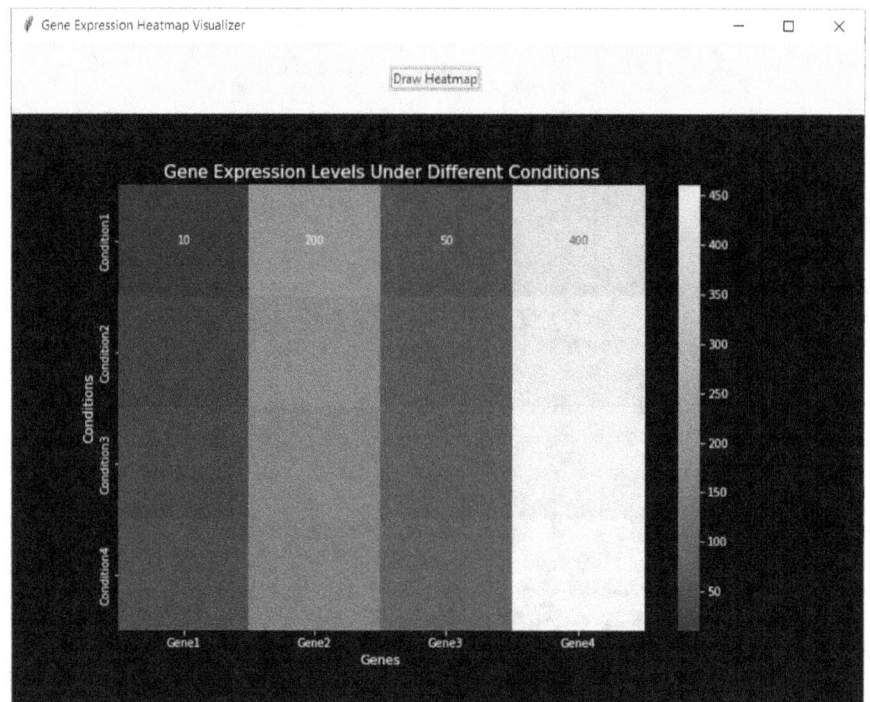

Features of the GUI

- Interactive Data Visualization: Users can interactively visualize gene expression data through dynamically generated heatmaps, providing a clear and intuitive representation of complex biological data.

- Integration of Matplotlib and Seaborn with Tkinter: Seamlessly integrates advanced visualization libraries into the Tkinter application, allowing for sophisticated data visualizations within the GUI.
- Real-Time Feedback: Provides immediate visual updates upon user interaction, enhancing the usability and responsiveness of the GUI.

This GUI application serves as an effective tool for biologists, geneticists, or data analysts, offering advanced visualization capabilities for gene expression analysis and making it ideal for presentations, educational purposes, or detailed scientific analysis.

Example 3.7
Analyzing Signal Data from Multiple Sensors

In signal processing, dictionaries are frequently used to manage and manipulate data efficiently. Here's a practical example where a Python dictionary is used to store, process, and analyze signal data from multiple sensors. This example might involve handling time-series data from different sensors, calculating the Fast Fourier Transform (FFT) of each signal, and storing both the original signals and their FFT results for analysis.

Scenario
Imagine we're working with a system that has multiple sensors collecting vibration data from machinery. We want to monitor the frequency components of these signals to identify unusual patterns that could indicate potential mechanical failures.

Step-by-Step Guide
1. Data Collection

Each sensor's data is stored in a dictionary, where the keys are sensor identifiers and the values are lists representing the signal data (e.g., vibration measurements taken over time).

2. Signal Processing

We compute the FFT of each signal to analyze the frequency components. This is useful in many engineering applications for spectral analysis.

3. Data Storage and Analysis

We store both the original time-series data and the FFT results in a dictionary for further analysis, possibly including visualization or automated alerts for anomalies.

Python Code Example

Here's how you might implement this in Python:

```python
import numpy as np
import matplotlib.pyplot as plt

# Simulating signal data collection
sensors_data = {
    "sensor1": np.random.normal(0, 1, 1024),  # Normal distribution data simulating sensor signals
    "sensor2": np.random.normal(0, 1, 1024),
    "sensor3": np.random.normal(0, 1, 1024)
}

# Function to compute FFT of a signal
def compute_fft(signal):
    n = len(signal)
    fft_data = np.fft.fft(signal)
    fft_freq = np.fft.fftfreq(n)
    return fft_freq, np.abs(fft_data)

# Dictionary to store FFT results
fft_results = {}

# Processing each sensor's data
for sensor, data in sensors_data.items():
    frequencies, fft_data = compute_fft(data)
    fft_results[sensor] = {
        "frequencies": frequencies,
        "fft": fft_data
    }

# Example: Plotting the FFT of one sensor
def plot_fft(sensor_id):
    fft_data = fft_results[sensor_id]
    plt.figure(figsize=(10, 4))
    plt.plot(fft_data["frequencies"], fft_data["fft"])
    plt.title(f"FFT of {sensor_id}")
    plt.xlabel("Frequency (Hz)")
    plt.ylabel("Amplitude")
    plt.grid(True)
    plt.show()

# Plot FFT for 'sensor1'
plot_fft("sensor1")
```

Explanation
1. Data Collection: Simulated sensor data is generated using random numbers. Each sensor has a unique key in the sensors_data dictionary.
2. Signal Processing: The compute_fft function is used to calculate the FFT of the signal data. The FFT (Fast Fourier Transform) is a powerful tool to analyze the frequency components of a signal, which is crucial in many fields such as audio processing, telecommunications, and bioinformatics.
3. Data Storage: FFT results are stored in another dictionary called fft_results, which uses sensor IDs as keys. Each entry stores both the frequency bins (frequencies) and the magnitude of the FFT (fft).
4. Visualization: The plot_fft function visualizes the frequency spectrum of a selected sensor. This visual representation helps in analyzing the predominant frequencies in the signal, which can be critical for diagnosing issues like mechanical faults.

This example encapsulates how dictionaries in Python can serve as an efficient and flexible data structure for handling complex signal processing tasks, enabling easy manipulation, storage, and retrieval of structured data such as time-series measurements from sensors.

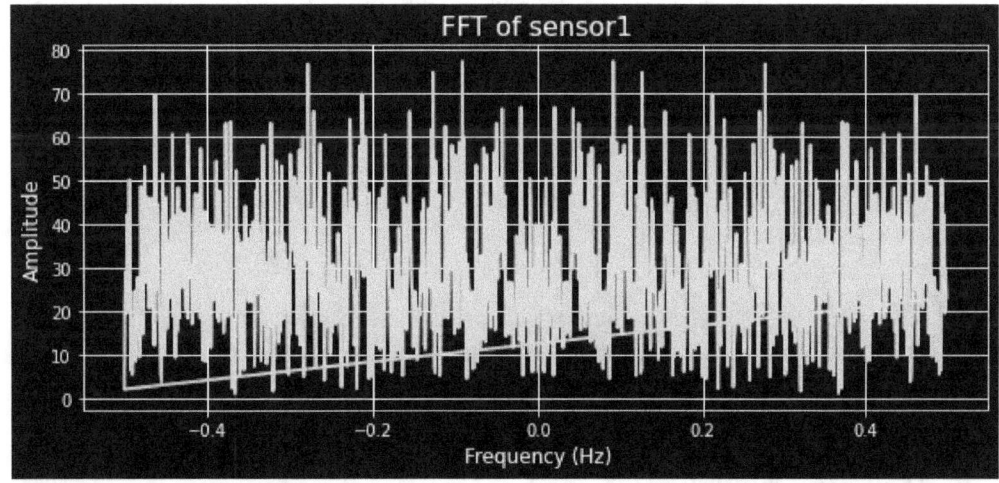

Example 3.8
GUI Tkinter for Analyzing Signal Data from Multiple Sensors

To create the script that processes and plots the Fast Fourier Transform (FFT) of simulated sensor data into a rich, interactive real-time graphical user interface (GUI) using Tkinter, we will encapsulate the functionality into a GUI application. This application will allow users to select a sensor and dynamically view its FFT plot.

Step-by-Step Guide to Building the GUI:
Step 1: Import Required Libraries
We'll need tkinter for the GUI, numpy for handling numerical operations, and matplotlib for plotting. We'll also use matplotlib.backends.backend_tkagg to embed matplotlib figures in the Tkinter window.

Step 2: Design the GUI Layout
The GUI will have a dropdown menu to select the sensor and a button to generate the FFT plot for the selected sensor. The plot will be dynamically displayed within the Tkinter window.

Step 3: Implement Functionality
Convert functions into methods of a GUI class, manage sensor data and FFT results as class attributes, and update the plot based on user interaction.

Python Code Example:

```python
import tkinter as tk
from tkinter import ttk
import numpy as np
import matplotlib.pyplot as plt
from matplotlib.backends.backend_tkagg import FigureCanvasTkAgg
from matplotlib.figure import Figure

class FFTVisualizerApp:
    def __init__(self, master):
        self.master = master
        self.master.title("FFT Visualizer")
        self.master.geometry("800x600")

        # Initializing data
        self.sensors_data = {
            "sensor1": np.random.normal(0, 1, 1024),
            "sensor2": np.random.normal(0, 1, 1024),
```

```python
            "sensor3": np.random.normal(0, 1, 1024)
        }
        self.fft_results = self.compute_all_ffts()

        # GUI Components
        self.setup_widgets()

    def setup_widgets(self):
        self.sensor_var = tk.StringVar()
        self.sensor_selector = ttk.Combobox(self.master, textvariable=self.sensor_var,
                                            values=list(self.sensors_data.keys()))
        self.sensor_selector.pack(pady=20)

        self.plot_button       =        ttk.Button(self.master,       text="Plot       FFT",
command=self.plot_selected_fft)
        self.plot_button.pack(pady=10)

        self.figure = Figure(figsize=(10, 4), dpi=100)
        self.canvas = FigureCanvasTkAgg(self.figure, self.master)
        self.canvas_widget = self.canvas.get_tk_widget()
        self.canvas_widget.pack(fill=tk.BOTH, expand=True)

    def compute_all_ffts(self):
        fft_results = {}
        for sensor, data in self.sensors_data.items():
            frequencies, fft_data = self.compute_fft(data)
            fft_results[sensor] = {"frequencies": frequencies, "fft": fft_data}
        return fft_results

    def compute_fft(self, signal):
        n = len(signal)
        fft_data = np.fft.fft(signal)
        fft_freq = np.fft.fftfreq(n)
        return fft_freq, np.abs(fft_data)

    def plot_selected_fft(self):
        sensor_id = self.sensor_var.get()
        if sensor_id:
            fft_data = self.fft_results[sensor_id]
            self.figure.clear()
            ax = self.figure.add_subplot(111)
            ax.plot(fft_data["frequencies"], fft_data["fft"])
            ax.set_title(f"FFT of {sensor_id}")
            ax.set_xlabel("Frequency (Hz)")
            ax.set_ylabel("Amplitude")
            ax.grid(True)
            self.canvas.draw()

if __name__ == "__main__":
    root = tk.Tk()
```

```
app = FFTVisualizerApp(root)
root.mainloop()
```

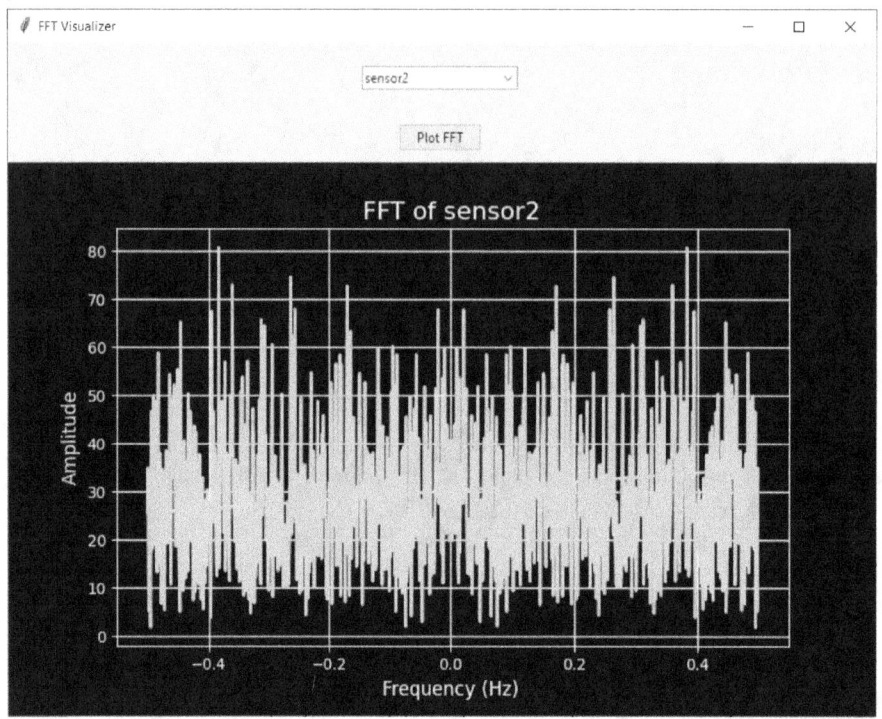

Explanation of the Code:
1. Class Initialization (__init__): Sets up the main window and initializes sensor data and FFT results.
2. Widget Setup (setup_widgets): Creates a dropdown menu for sensor selection, a button to trigger FFT plotting, and a canvas to display the plot.
3. FFT Computation (compute_all_ffts, compute_fft): Calculates FFT for all sensors once and stores results to avoid recomputation.
4. Plot Functionality (plot_selected_fft): Handles plotting the FFT for the selected sensor when the button is clicked.

Features of the GUI:
- Interactive Selection: Users can choose which sensor's data to plot using a dropdown menu.
- Real-Time Data Visualization: The FFT plot updates dynamically based on the user's selection, providing immediate visual feedback.

Integration of Scientific Computing with GUI: Combines numpy and matplotlib functionalities seamlessly within a Tkinter application, suitable for real-world applications in data analysis, signal processing, and more.

Example 3.9
Handling Parameter Tuning

In the realm of data science, dictionaries are invaluable for handling structured data, managing configurations, parameter tuning, and data aggregation. Below, I'll provide a detailed real-world example that showcases how a dictionary can be used in a machine learning project to manage hyperparameters for model tuning. This example involves using Python and popular machine learning libraries to demonstrate a practical application.

Scenario: Machine Learning Model Tuning

Imagine you're working on a machine learning project where you need to tune the hyperparameters of a classification model to achieve optimal performance. We'll use the random forest classifier as our model and tune its parameters using a dictionary.

Example: Tuning Hyperparameters with Scikit-Learn
Step 1: Import Required Libraries
We'll use scikit-learn for building the model and pandas for data handling.

```
import numpy as np
import pandas as pd
from sklearn.ensemble import RandomForestClassifier
from sklearn.model_selection import train_test_split, GridSearchCV
from sklearn.metrics import accuracy_score
```

Step 2: Prepare the Dataset
Let's assume we have a dataset loaded into a pandas DataFrame. For simplicity, we'll simulate loading a dataset.

```
# Simulate some data
np.random.seed(0)
data = np.random.rand(100, 5)
target = np.random.randint(0, 2, 100)

# Load data into a DataFrame
df = pd.DataFrame(data, columns=[f'Feature_{i}' for i in range(1, 6)])
```

```
df['Target'] = target
```

Step 3: Setup Training and Test Sets
Split the data into training and test sets to evaluate the model performance.

```
X = df.drop('Target', axis=1)
y = df['Target']
X_train, X_test, y_train, y_test = train_test_split(X, y, test_size=0.25,
random_state=42)
```

Step 4: Define a Dictionary for Hyperparameters
Use a dictionary to specify the hyperparameter grid for tuning.

```
param_grid = {
    'n_estimators': [50, 100, 200],
    'max_features': ['auto', 'sqrt', 'log2'],
    'max_depth': [None, 10, 20, 30],
    'criterion': ['gini', 'entropy']
}
```

Step 5: Model Tuning with GridSearchCV
Use GridSearchCV to find the best hyperparameters from the defined grid.

```
# Initialize the classifier
rf = RandomForestClassifier(random_state=42)

# Grid search for hyperparameter tuning
grid_search = GridSearchCV(estimator=rf, param_grid=param_grid, cv=5, verbose=1,
scoring='accuracy')
grid_search.fit(X_train, y_train)

# Best parameters and best score
print("Best parameters:", grid_search.best_params_)
print("Best cross-validation score: {:.2f}".format(grid_search.best_score_))
```

Step 6: Evaluate the Model
Finally, evaluate the best model on the test set.

```
best_model = grid_search.best_estimator_
predictions = best_model.predict(X_test)
print("Test set accuracy: {:.2f}".format(accuracy_score(y_test, predictions)))
```

Explanation
1. Hyperparameter Dictionary: This dictionary is crucial as it defines the space over which to search for the best model parameters. Each key corresponds to a hyperparameter name, and the values are lists of settings to try.
2. Model Training: GridSearchCV systematically works through multiple combinations of parameter options, cross-validating as it goes to determine which tune gives the best performance.
3. Model Evaluation: Finally, we test the best-found model on unseen data to evaluate its performance.

Conclusion

This real-world example demonstrates how dictionaries in Python can be effectively used to manage model configurations in data science projects. Dictionaries provide a flexible and efficient way to organize hyperparameters for model tuning, making the code more modular, readable, and easier to modify or extend. Such approaches are critical in professional data science environments where model performance can significantly impact business outcomes.

Example 3.10
GUI Tkinter for Handling Parameter Tuning

To develop a rich, real-time GUI using Tkinter that allows for interactive tuning of RandomForest hyperparameters, we can create a user interface that includes comboboxes or textboxes for each hyperparameter. This GUI will provide an intuitive way for users to select values, initiate a grid search, and view the results directly within the application.

Here's how to set up the GUI:
Step 1: Import Necessary Libraries

```
import tkinter as tk
from tkinter import ttk
import numpy as np
import pandas as pd
from sklearn.ensemble import RandomForestClassifier
from sklearn.model_selection import train_test_split, GridSearchCV
from sklearn.metrics import accuracy_score
```

Step 2: Define the GUI Class

```python
class RandomForestTuner(tk.Tk):
    def __init__(self):
        super().__init__()
        self.title("Random Forest Hyperparameter Tuning")
        self.geometry("500x400")

        # Data Preparation
        np.random.seed(0)
        data = np.random.rand(100, 5)
        target = np.random.randint(0, 2, 100)
        df = pd.DataFrame(data, columns=[f'Feature_{i}' for i in range(1, 6)])
        df['Target'] = target
        X = df.drop('Target', axis=1)
        y = df['Target']
        self.X_train, self.X_test, self.y_train, self.y_test = train_test_split(X, y, test_size=0.25, random_state=42)

        # UI Components
        self.create_widgets()

    def create_widgets(self):
        # Parameters with options
        self.params = {
            'n_estimators': ['50', '100', '200'],  # Convert integers to strings for combobox compatibility
            'max_features': ['sqrt', 'log2'],
            'max_depth': ['None', '10', '20', '30'],  # Including 'None' as a string option
            'criterion': ['gini', 'entropy']
        }

        self.inputs = {}
        row = 0
        for param, options in self.params.items():
            ttk.Label(self, text=param).grid(row=row, column=0, padx=10, sticky='w')
            current_var = tk.StringVar()
            combobox = ttk.Combobox(self, textvariable=current_var, values=options, state="readonly")
            combobox.grid(row=row, column=1, padx=10, pady=5, sticky='ew')
            self.inputs[param] = current_var
            if param == 'max_depth':
                current_var.set('None')  # Set default to 'None' for max_depth
            row += 1

        # Button to execute Grid Search
        ttk.Button(self, text="Run Grid Search", command=self.run_grid_search).grid(row=row, padx=10, pady=20, sticky='ew')
```

```
        # Label to show results
        self.result_label = ttk.Label(self, text="")
        self.result_label.grid(row=row+1, padx=10, pady=10, sticky='ew')

    def run_grid_search(self):
        # Proper dictionary comprehension that fixes the scope of 'param'
        param_grid = {
            param:              [int(self.inputs[param].get())              if
self.inputs[param].get().isdigit()
                    else self.inputs[param].get() if self.inputs[param].get() !=
'None'
                    else None] for param in self.params
        }
        rf = RandomForestClassifier(random_state=42)
        grid_search   =   GridSearchCV(estimator=rf,   param_grid=param_grid,   cv=5,
verbose=1, scoring='accuracy')
        grid_search.fit(self.X_train, self.y_train)

        best_params = grid_search.best_params_
        best_score = grid_search.best_score_
        best_model = grid_search.best_estimator_
        predictions = best_model.predict(self.X_test)
        accuracy = accuracy_score(self.y_test, predictions)

        result_text = f"Best Params: {best_params}\nCV Score: {best_score:.2f}\nTest
Accuracy: {accuracy:.2f}"
        self.result_label.config(text=result_text)


if __name__ == "__main__":
    app = RandomForestTuner()
    app.mainloop()
```

Explanation of the Code

- Class Initialization: Set up the main window and initialize data preparation steps.
- Widget Creation: Dynamically create input widgets based on predefined hyperparameters. Users can input or select parameters directly through the GUI.
- Grid Search Execution: Implement the functionality to run the grid search based on user inputs, and display the best parameters, cross-validation score, and test set accuracy.

Features of the GUI
- Dynamic Parameter Configuration: The GUI allows users to configure RandomForest hyperparameters dynamically.
- Real-time Results Display: Immediately display the results of the grid search within the GUI.
- User-friendly Interface: Provides a simple and intuitive interface for users to interact with machine learning model tuning.

This approach enhances the usability of machine learning models by making hyperparameter tuning more accessible and interactive. It is an excellent tool for educational purposes, demonstrations, and even for professional use where quick parameter tuning is required.

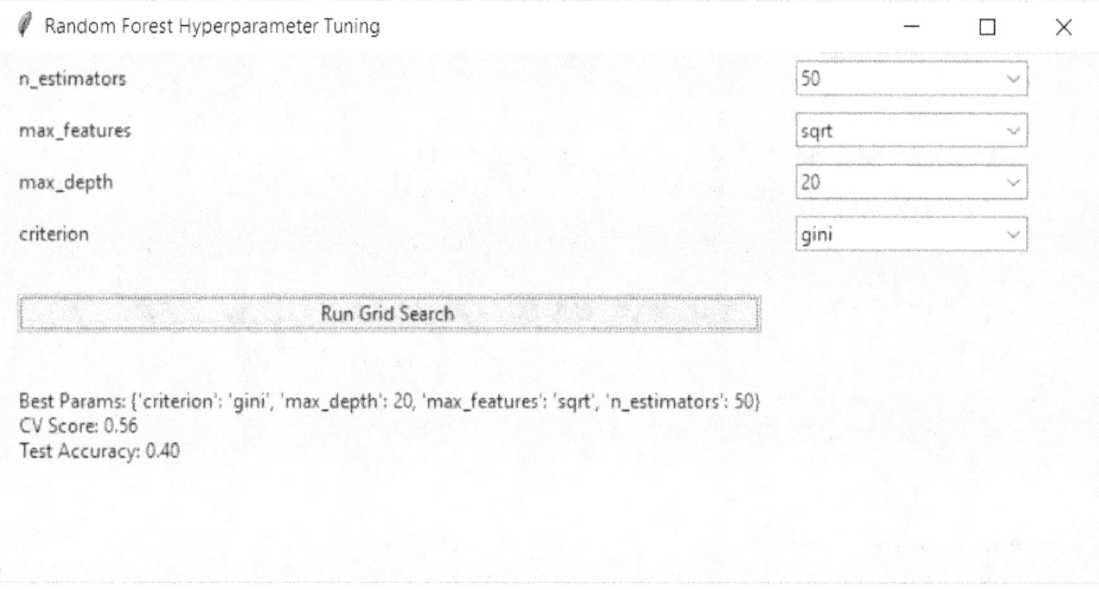

Bibliography

Vivian Siahaan and Rismon Hasiholan Sianipar. *TKINTER, DATA SCIENCE, AND MACHINE LEARNING*. North Sumatera: Balige Publishing, 2023.

Vivian Siahaan and Rismon Hasiholan Sianipar. *DATA VISUALIZATION, TIME-SERIES FORECASTING, AND PREDICTION USING MACHINE LEARNING WITH TKINTER*. North Sumatera: Balige Publishing, 2023.

Vivian Siahaan and Rismon Hasiholan Sianipar. *TIME-SERIES WEATHER FORECASTING AND PREDICTION USING MACHINE LEARNING WITH TKINTER*. North Sumatera: Balige Publishing, 2023.

Vivian Siahaan and Rismon Hasiholan Sianipar. DATA VISUALIZATION, TIME-SERIES FORECASTING, AND PREDICTION USING MACHINE LEARNING WITH TKINTER. North Sumatera: Balige Publishing, 2023.

Vivian Siahaan and Rismon Hasiholan Sianipar. START FROM SCRATCH DIGITAL SIGNAL PROCESSING WITH TKINTER. North Sumatera: Balige Publishing, 2023.

Vivian Siahaan and Rismon Hasiholan Sianipar. START FROM SCRATCH DIGITAL IMAGE PROCESSING WITH TKINTER. North Sumatera: Balige Publishing, 2023.

Vivian Siahaan and Rismon Hasiholan Sianipar. START FROM SCRATCH DIGITAL IMAGE PROCESSING WITH TKINTER. North Sumatera: Balige Publishing, 2023.

Vivian Siahaan and Rismon Hasiholan Sianipar. IMAGE DENOISING, EDGE DETECTION, AND SEGMENTATION WITH TKINTER. North Sumatera: Balige Publishing, 2023.

Vivian Siahaan and Rismon Hasiholan Sianipar. DIGITAL VIDEO PROCESSING PROJECTS USING PYTHON AND TKINTER. North Sumatera: Balige Publishing, 2024.

Vivian Siahaan and Rismon Hasiholan Sianipar. FRAME ANALYSIS AND PROCESSING IN DIGITAL VIDEO USING PYTHON AND TKINTER. North Sumatera: Balige Publishing, 2024.

Vivian Siahaan and Rismon Hasiholan Sianipar. MOTION ANALYSIS AND OBJECT TRACKING USING PYTHON AND TKINTER. North Sumatera: Balige Publishing, 2024.

Vivian Siahaan and Rismon Hasiholan Sianipar. FRAME FILTERING AND EDGES-DETECTION USING PYTHON AND TKINTER. North Sumatera: Balige Publishing, 2024.

Vivian Siahaan and Rismon Hasiholan Sianipar. OPTICAL FLOW ANALYSIS AND MOTION ESTIMATION IN DIGITAL VIDEO WITH PYTHON AND TKINTER. North Sumatera: Balige Publishing, 2024.

Vivian Siahaan and Rismon Hasiholan Sianipar. GRADIENT-BASED BLOCK MATCHING MOTION ESTIMATION AND OBJECT TRACKING WITH PYTHON AND TKINTER. North Sumatera: Balige Publishing, 2024.

Vivian Siahaan and Rismon Hasiholan Sianipar. FEATURES-BASED MOTION ESTIMATION AND OBJECT TRACKING WITH PYTHON AND TKINTER. North Sumatera: Balige Publishing, 2024.